A Revolutionary War Road Trip on US Route 9W

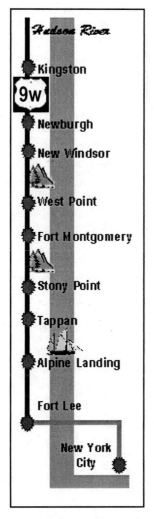

Spend A Revolutionary Day Along One of America's Most Historic Routes

OTHER REVOLUTIONARY WAR ROAD TRIPS
BY RAYMOND C. HOUGHTON

A Revolutionary War Road Trip on US Route 4
(Castleton, VT to Albany, NY)

A Revolutionary War Road Trip on US Route 7
(Pittsfield, MA to Burlington, VT)

A Revolutionary War Road Trip on US Route 9
(Kings Ferry, NY to Saratoga Springs, NY)

A Revolutionary War Road Trip on US Route 202
(Elks Neck, MD to Philadelphia, PA)

A Revolutionary War Boat Trip on the Champlain Canal
(Bethlehem, NY to Basin Harbor, VT)

A Revolutionary War Road Trip on US Route 20
(Albany, NY to Boston, MA, in preparation)

A Revolutionary War Road Trip on US Route 60
(Charlottesville, VA to Yorktown, VA, in preparation)

A Revolutionary War Road Trip on the Mohawk Turnpike
(Oswego, NY to Schenectady, NY, in preparation)

A Revolutionary War Road Trip on US Route 221
(Chesnee, SC to Augusta, GA, in preparation)

A Revolutionary War Road Trip on US Route 9W

Spend a Revolutionary Day Along
One of America's Most Historic Routes

Raymond C. Houghton

Cyber Haus
Delmar, NY

A Revolutionary War Road Trip on US Route 9W
Spend A Revolutionary Day Along
One of America's Most Historic Routes

Revolutionary War Road Trips
are published by Cyber Haus
and printed on-demand
by Booksurge, LLC,
www.booksurge.com,
1-866-308-6235.

ISBN: 1-931373-11-6

Cyber Haus
159 Delaware Avenue, #145
Delmar, NY 12054
http://www.cyhaus.com/
Http://www.revolutionaryday.com/
cyhaus@msn.com
518-478-9798

To my Mother-in-Law,
Monica Dugan Laws,
a native Kingstonian

INTRODUCTION

US Route 9W goes from New Jersey to Upstate New York paralleling the Hudson River along its west bank, passing through the Highlands of New York and skirting the east side of the Catskill Mountains. There are many historic areas to discover and explore along this route — history that covers the entire American Revolution from 1775 to 1783. This book presents a one-day, road trip through these areas, but be warned — with so much to see, it could easily take a week.

There were many heated exchanges along the Hudson River between American forces and British forces. In 1777, George Washington worried that "the loss of the Highland passes would open the navigation of the river, and enable the enemy, with facility, to throw their force into Albany, get into the rear of General Gates, and either oblige him to retreat, or put him between two fires." Fortunately for General Gates, the "fire" to his north was put out with a victory at Saratoga and the "fire" to his south was halted near Kingston. In 1778, Washington fortified the Highlands at West Point and, for the most part, kept the British

bottled-up in New York City for the remainder of the war.

A **Revolutionary Day** along historic US Route 9W begins early in the morning in New York City about thirteen miles south of the start of US Route 9W. New York City is where the battle for control of the Hudson began in 1775 and sets the stage for the sites that will be visited during the rest of the day.

From New York City, the road trip goes north along Route 9A to the George Washington Bridge and

crosses the Hudson to Fort Lee, New Jersey. In November 1776, Washington was forced to watch from Fort Lee as about 3,000 of his men on the opposite side of the Hudson succumb to heavy fire from about 15,000 British troops.

From Fort Lee, the road trip continues north to Alpine Landing then to Tappan, George Washington's Headquarters on four separate occasions. From Tappan, the road trip continues north to Stony Point, the site of a daring midnight assault by Americans in 1779. After Stony Point, the road trip follows Route 9W to Fort Montgomery and then to West Point, home of the United States Military Academy. Many of the fortifications and weapons used by the American forces to protect the Hudson River still remain today at West Point.

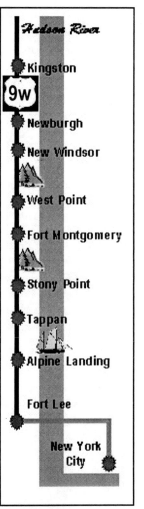

From West Point, the road trip continues north to New Windsor, the final encampment for the American forces, and then to Washington's final headquarters at Newburgh. He would spend almost 18 months at this headquarters — more time than he would spend at any other headquarters throughout the war.

From Newburgh, the road trip continues north on Route 9W and concludes in Kingston. In 1777, the British would torch the city, but many Revolutionary War era, stone homes still stand today in the Kingston Stockade.

TABLE OF CONTENTS & TRIP LOG

New York City: A short walk from Battery Park to Wall Street historically traverses the beginning and the end of the American Revolution as well as the beginning of the American nation.

New York City to Fort Lee: Travel up Route 9A and across the George Washington Bridge to Fort Lee.

Fort Lee: Visit the "post on the New Jersey side" where George Washington was forced to watch the surrender of New York City to the British.

Fort Lee to Alpine Landing: Rendezvous with Route 9W north.

Alpine Landing: Visit the base of the Palisades near the location of the British landing prior to the attack on Fort Lee.

Alpine Landing to Tappan: Cross over US Route 9W on the Palisades Parkway and make a quick stop at the state lookout.

NEW YORK CITY, NEW YORK

Battery Park — In August of 1775, King George III declared that the colonies are in a state of "open and avowed rebellion." During the same time period, the New York Provincial Congress knew that the cannons in Battery Park were at risk and should be secured. Under orders of the congress and at night, Captain John Lamb with about sixty men began dismantling them. The British ship, the HMS Asia, under the command of Captain George Vandeput detected the activity and sent a barge-load of men to investigate. After a warning shot was fired from the barge, Lamb's men returned fire, killing one of the men on the barge. In retaliation, the HMS Asia open fired on the battery.

This opening volley marked the beginning of hostilities on the Hudson. The event caused major panic in New

---

Castle Clinton National Monument

Last of a series of forts which from the Dutch settlement of 1624, guarded lower Manhattan, this structure was built by the United States in the years 1808 to 1811. It was first called "West Battery," and was one of the important defenses of New York Harbor during the War of 1812 period. Named in honor of Gov. DeWitt Clinton in 1815, in that year it was made Headquarters, US Third Military District. From 1816 to 1820 Gen. Winfield Scott was in command. The Headquarters was removed from Castle Clinton to Governors Island in 1820.

National Park Service
United States
Department of Interior

(Castle Clinton Marker)

York City and demonstrated how easily the city could be attacked from the harbor.

Although the only historic remains that can be found in today's Battery Park date back to the War of 1812, an early morning walk along the water's edge clearly shows its strategic importance. Walk from the west side of the park near Fort Clinton and go east. One can see the Hudson River with the New Jersey Coast in the distance, as well as, Ellis Island and the Statue of Liberty. Continue walking to the east. One can see the

East River with Staten Island, Governor's Island and Long Island in the distance.

The British occupied much of what can be seen from Battery Park for the better part of the Revolutionary War, including Battery Park itself and the area occupied by the buildings that can be seen to the north.

Fraunces Tavern — The tavern can be reached by taking one of the walkways at the eastern end of Battery Park north toward the city and proceeding up

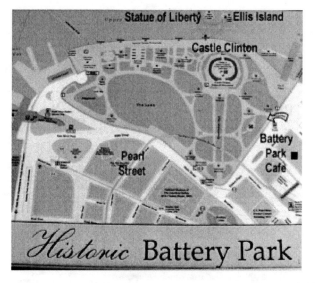

Pearl Street near Starbucks Coffee to the intersection with Broad Street. Fraunces Tavern is at this intersection.

In the short distance from Battery Park to Fraunces Tavern, one historically traverses the beginning of the Revolutionary War in 1775 to the end of the war in 1783.

Built in 1719 as a residence, and later turned into a tavern, Fraunces Tavern has played a part in events before, during and after the American Revolution:

Fraunces Tavern

After the American Revolutionary War, on December 4, 1783, General George Washington bade an emotional farewell to his officers at a banquet held in the Long Room, located on the second floor of this tavern. Samuel Fraunces, a West Indian innkeeper, was the proprietor; he later became Washington's chief steward. Fraunces, also an American patriot, was host to secret meetings of the Sons of Liberty and gave aid to American prisoners of war. The present building, purchased by the Sons of the Revolution in 1904, was restored by them on this site and has since been maintained by them.

Plaque provided by the
New York Community Trust, 1976

(Fraunces Tavern Marker)

Washington's Farewell to his Officers
by Alonzo Chappel

Before the Revolution, Stephen Delancey and his family enjoyed the life of a prosperous mercantile family in an elite New York City neighborhood.

Later, ambitious entrepreneur Samuel Fraunces established one of the finest dining and drinking establishments in New York City, and George Washington became a frequent guest.

Rebels met and planned what would become the American Revolution, while being served by tavern-keeper Samuel Fraunces.

George Washington wept as he bade farewell to his officers in 1783, at the close of the Revolution, in the tavern's Long Room.

After the Revolution, John Jay, the Secretary of Foreign Affairs, and Henry Knox, the Secretary of War, and the staff of the Department of Treasury, worked and made decisions that affected the direction of the new nation, when the federal government rented the tavern as cabinet offices from 1785 to 1787.

Today, Fraunces Tavern is a museum that was founded in 1907. It is dedicated to the study and interpretation of early American history and culture. They offer changing exhibitions, period rooms, tours, public programs and publications. The Long Room is now an example of a late 18th century tavern dining room. The Davis Center displays colorful reproduction, Revolutionary War flags. Special events are held on George Washington's Birthday, Flag Day and the Fourth of July.

Federal Hall — The hall is at the intersection of Broad Street and Wall street, about five blocks north of Fraunces Tavern just past the New York Stock Exchange. The original Federal Hall that stood here during the 18th century was the first capital building of the United States and the location where George Washington was sworn in as the first President of the United States.

On Federal Hall is an engraving that shows a p r a y i n g G e o r g e Washington. The engraving reminds us that Washington was a person who was not above asking for God's blessings and support. Although he is shown praying in solitude, he often asked his officers to join him in prayer.

Federal Hall National Memorial

A majestic statue of George Washington stands on the front steps of Federal Hall in memory of Washington's inauguration as the country's first president — which happened on this spot on April 30th, 1789. The current building is named for the original Federal Hall, perhaps the most historic site in the entire country, where two centuries ago American democracy was born. From 1785 to 1790, New York served as the first capital of the brand-new United States of America. It was in Federal Hall that Congress met for the first time, adopted the Bill of Rights, and created the Departments of State, War and Treasury, and the United States Supreme Court. Today, Federal Hall serves as a museum operated by the National Park Service.

Today's Federal Hall, built 1836-42 as the city's Custom House, is one of the few Wall Street buildings surviving from a time when the street was lined with new American banks pretending to be old Greek temples. Outside, its row of Parthenon-inspired columns suggests a reverence for Greek democracy; inside, it Pantheon-like dome brings to mind the economic power of the Roman Empire — neatly summarizing two dominant 19th-century American ideals.

(Federal Hall Marker)

In July 1776, John Page wrote:

> We know the race is not to the swift
> nor the battle to the strong.
> Do you not think an angel
> rides in the whirlwind and directs this storm?

This was John Page's explanation for the many Revolutionary War events where one is at a complete loss to explain the logic behind decisions that were made or events that took place. Many of these occurred along the banks of the Hudson River and are upcoming stops on this road trip. Could they have not been the answer to George Washington's prayers?

Also, on Federal Hall is an engraved plaque in the shape of the state of Ohio. Ohio was founded by circumstances created by the Revolution. One of the problems that Congress had throughout the war was raising funds to pay the soldiers. One of the ways they devised was to give them land in exchange for the money they were owed. As the marker explains, Ohio was founded by a group of soldiers who accepted this arrangement.

Ohio Company of Associates

On this site the United States in Congress assembled on the 13th day of July in the year of our lord 1787 and of their sovereignty and independence enacted an ordinance for the government of the territory northwest of the river Ohio, by which it was dedicated forever to freedom under another ordinance passed here by the same body on the 27th day of same month. Manasseh Cutler, acting for "The Ohio Company of Associates," an organization of soldiers of the Revolutionary Army, purchased from the Board of Treasury for settlement a portion of the waste and vacant land of the territory. On April 7th 1788, Rufus Putnam, heading a party of forty-eight, began the first settlement at Marietta, and on July 15th, Arthur St. Clair, as first governor, established civil government in the territory. From these beginnings sprang the states of Ohio, Indiana, Illinois, Michigan and Wisconsin.

(Federal Hall Marker)

Trinity Church — Anchoring the west end of Wall Street on Broadway is Trinity Church, which was chartered in 1697. From the entrance to the church one can get a peek at the beauty that lies inside. On the south side of the entrance to the church, there is a memorial to Alexander Hamilton and the many other officers of the Revolutionary War that are interred in the graveyard including Richard Montgomery and Horatio Gates, both Major Generals in the Continental Army. Alexander Hamilton's grave can be seen from Rector Street that is about a half block south on Broadway and another half block west on Rector Street:

Trinity Church

was first founded in the year 1696, enlarged and beautified in 1737, and entirely destroyed in the great Conflagration of the City, Sept. 21st AD 1776.

This building was erected on the Site of the former Church in the Year 1788.

Right Rev. Samuel Provost DD Rector
James Duane Esq., J. John Jay Esq. Churchwardens

(Trinity Church Marker)

- Alexander Hamilton began his involvement with the American Revolution while he was a student at King's College (now Columbia University). He formed an artillery company in 1775 and became the company commander when he was commissioned a Captain in 1776. He served under George Washington at the battles of Long Island,

Alexander Hamilton
by John Trumbull

Harlem Heights, Trenton and Princeton. In March 1777, at the age of 20, he was promoted to Lieutenant Colonel and became George Washington's Aide-de-Camp and served as Washington's trusted advisor for four and a half years. In July 1781, he served under Lafayette and participated in the siege at Yorktown. After the Revolution, Hamilton helped lead the efforts to

create a constitutional convention and served as the first Secretary of the Treasury under President Washington.

- Richard Montgomery was a veteran of the French and Indian War and was one of the first generals commissioned in the Continental Army. In 1775, he served under Philip Schuyler, the commander of the Northern Department of the Continental Army, in the expedition against British-held Quebec. When Schuyler became ill, he took command of the expedition and was killed leading a winter assault against the well-defended fortress of Quebec.

- Horatio Gates was also a veteran of the French and Indian War and was among the first generals commissioned in the Continental Army. He was popular with congress and they sent him to replace Schuyler as commander of the Northern

---

1783   1957

Erected by the
New York State Society of the Cincinnati

To the memory of Alexander Hamilton, 1757-1804
Lieutenant Colonel
Aide de Camp to General Washington

And those other officers of the Continental Army and Navy, original members of the Society, whose remains are interred in the church yards of the Trinity Parish.

(Trinity Church Marker)

Department of the Army after the American retreat from Fort Ticonderoga in 1777. He was in command during the Battles at Saratoga and was given credit for the victory. In 1780, congress made him commander of the Southern Department of the Army, but his reputation suffered after his flight from the battlefield at Camden, South Carolina, and he was replaced by General Nathaniel Greene. He later resurrected his reputation and rejoined Washington at Newburgh. After the Revolution, he served in the New York legislature.

Saint Paul's Chapel — If time permits, the chapel is among two other Revolutionary War sites that can be

St. Paul's Chapel was established by Trinity Church as a Chapel of Ease, a term which refers to a dependent church or chapel built to accommodate and expanding parish. Trinity, the Mother Church chartered in 1697, is located at Broadway and Wall Street. St. Paul's was consecrated October 30, 1766, "Esteemed one of the most elegant edifices on the continent...At 10 o'clock the civil and ecclesiastical officials walked in procession from Fort George to the chapel. The services include a sermon by Dr. Auchmuty and vocal instrumental music." (New York Gazette, November 3, 1766)

(St. Paul's Chapel Marker)

> On September 21, 1776, after the British had
> retaken New York, a fire of suspicious origin raged
> through lower Manhattan. Trinity Church was
> destroyed but St. Paul's Chapel survived. Until
> Trinity Church was rebuilt in 1792, St. Paul's
> served both congregations. "All that is West of the
> New Exchange, along Broad Street to the North
> River (Hudson River), as high as the City Hall, and
> from thence along the Broad Way and North River
> to King's College, is in Ruins. St. Paul's Church
> and the college were saved with the utmost
> difficulty...Poor Trinity Church, a principal object
> of republican independent malice was set on fire in
> three places" (St. James Church, November 7,
> 1776).
>
> (St. Paul's Chapel Exhibit)

found about five blocks north on Broadway. It was
built in 1766 and is the oldest public building in
Manhattan. During the Revolution, the church
remained fiercely loyal to the British Crown and was
spared the great "conflagration" of 1776 when the
British invaded the city.

After the war, George Washington attended services
here while New York City was the capital of the United

> Charles Inglis, Rector of Trinity Church (1777-
> 1783) remained loyal to the British Monarchy
> throughout the American Revolution. After his
> cause was lost, Inglis fled New York for Nova
> Scotia, Canada, where he became the first Anglican
> Bishop of the New World.
>
> (St. Paul's Chapel Exhibit)

States. A special service was held on his inauguration day, April 30, 1789.

The chapel, which is a block from the former site of the World Trade Center, became a sanctuary after the 2001

The human spirit is not measured by the size of the act, but by the size of the heart.

(World Trade Center Exhibit)

George Washington's Prayer

Almighty God, we make our earnest prayer that Thou will wilt keep the United States in Thy holy protection; that Thou wilt incline the hearts of the citizens to cultivate a spirit of subordination and obedience to government; to entertain a brotherly affection and love for one another and for their fellow citizens of the United States at large; and finally that Thou wilt most graciously be pleased to dispose us all to do justice, to love mercy, and to demean ourselves with that charity, humility and pacific temper of mind, which were the characteristics of the Devine Author of our blessed religion, and without an humble imitation of whose example in these things can never hope to be a happy nation. Grant our supplication we beseech Thee, through Jesus Christ our Lord, Amen.

Presented by the Women's Committee of the George Washington-Bulgrave Institution, February 22, 1926.

(Saint Paul's Chapel Marker)

attack on the Twin Towers. Today, the chapel is also a memorial to the sacrifice made by the 911 firefighters, police and other public servants and volunteers.

City Hall Park — About a block further north of St. Paul's is City Hall Park. During the war, this area was the home of thousands of American prisoners. Conditions in the prisons were atrocious. Some were so over-crowded that all could not lie down and sleep at the same time.

In front of city hall is a statue of Nathan Hale. He was an American spy assigned to New York City after the Battle Long Island. He volunteered for the job at the

---

Nathan Hale
City Hall Park

"I only regret that I have but one life to lose for my country."

This graceful, 13-foot standing bronze figure, sculpted by Frederick Max Monnics (1863-1937), directly faces City Hall and honors the last moments of the 21-year-old American Revolutionary era spy, Nathan Hale (1755-1776).

Disguised as a Dutch schoolteacher, Hale attempted to infiltrate New York's British ranks to gather intelligence on the enemy's Long Island military installations. The young man was captured, however, on the night of September 21, 1776 and hanged for treason the next morning on gallows believed to have been erected near 63rd Street and First Avenue...

(New York City Marker)

---

request of George Washington. Hale disguised himself as a Dutch schoolmaster and slipped behind British lines. On September 21, 1776, he was recognized by a New Hampshire relative, the Tory Samuel Hale. Official papers found on his person revealed him as a spy and

the next morning he was led to the gallows. His final famous words: "I only regret that I have but one life to lose for my country."

Bowling Green — On your return to Battery Park on Broadway, Bowling Green is about two blocks south of Trinity Church. In 1770, after the British Parliament repealed the Townshend Tax, the colonists of New York, in celebration, erected a statue of King George III at Bowling Green. Six years later, the statue would become raw material for the making of bullets. It was pulled down by soldiers after George Washington had the Declaration of Independence read to them on July 9, 1776.

A short distance from Bowling Green was Fort George. The fort was built to protect the harbor but had little effect against the British Navy. After the British evacuated the city, the American flag was raised at the fort with a 13-gun salute. That evening, a fireworks display was reported to "exceed every former exhibition in the United States."

Breakfast in New York City — The Battery Park Café can be found at 2 Washington Street, just off Battery Place on the northeast side of Battery Park. For breakfast, they feature several breakfast  "platers" and the coffee is great.

New York City

New York City, capital of the Province of New York and focal point of the British strategy on the lower Hudson in 1776, was a small provincial city at the extreme southern tip of Manhattan Island. It extended from the Battery to what is now City Hall Park. In 1771, its population was only 21,863. It flourished on mercantile trade. Many of its inhabitants were of Dutch ancestry and still spoke the native tongue.

(Fort Lee Visitor Center Display)

NEW YORK CITY TO FORT LEE

Mile Mark 0.0 — Go west on Battery Place and turn right onto West Street, which is Route 9A, also called the West Side Highway.

Route 9A follows the same general route that some of the American forces under the command of George Washington would use on August 30, 1776 to retreat from the British who were just across the East River on Long Island. The day before, Washington's Army was on Long Island with its back against the East River. They were completely surrounded and outnumbered by the British who could have easily achieved victory two days earlier on August 28th, but General William Howe, Commander of the British forces, had inexplicably halted the British attack. On the next day when the British were ready to capture the Americans, the attack was delayed by a fierce "whirlwind" — a nor'easter storm (nor'easters are unusual in the summer). On the evening of the 29th, Washington left the campfires burning while he ferried the entire army across the East river under the cover of a heavy fog. He

Retreat at Long Island
by M. A. Wageman

reported that the fog seemed "to settle in a peculiar manner over both encampments".

Mile Mark 0.5 — Pass the former location of the World Trade Center. Two hundred and twenty-five years after the American escape from Manhattan, the West Side Highway would once again be an escape route for Americans under attack by terrorists on September 11, 2001.

Mile Mark 1.4 — Pass Canal Street. On the left you can see the towers that supply air to the Lincoln Tunnel which goes under the Hudson River.

Mile Mark 4.2 — Reach 44th Street and the home of the Intrepid World War II Naval Museum on the left.

Mile Mark 4.9 — Reach the last light on Route 9A and a ramp that takes you onto the elevated Hudson Parkway. The average speed to this point is a stop-and-

Britain's New York Strategy

The story of Fort Lee is interwoven into that of the New York campaign of 1776 for control of the lower Hudson River. For generations, the Hudson had occupied a position of strategic importance in the colonial wars fought between England and France. Connecting by means of portage with Lakes George and Champlain and the St. Lawrence River, the Hudson had long served as an important inland route of communication, travel, and invasion between the Atlantic Ocean and Canada.

Americans and Britons were aware that possession of the Hudson and the northern lakes would be crucial in the war which broke out in 1775. The British realized that if the line of the river and the lakes could be occupied and held, the colonies would be separated and their ability to wage war would be severely curtailed. They could then be individually subjugated or forced to surrender. The Americans also realized this, and made every effort to preserve the line of the river to their cause.

It was obvious that if the British could seize New York and the mouth of the Hudson they would be in position to push north along the waterway with ships of the Royal Navy. In 1775 and early 1776, while the American siege of Boston was still in progress, Washington and other American leaders realized that the next British move would be directed against New York by sea.

Only the lack of bold military leadership by General William Howe, the British commander-in-chief, was to deny the British the decisive victory to crush the rebellion which they could have attained at New York in the summer and autumn of 1776.

(Fort Lee Visitor Center Display)

American Defense Efforts

The American defense of New York City and the vital estuary of the Hudson in 1776 was difficult without adequate naval support. It was a city which could not be properly defended without a supporting fleet. Every military position on land could be easily flanked or threatened by means of the waterways which honeycombed the area, of which the British, with vast naval superiority, could take full advantage.

Apart from a small assortment of row galleys and river and coastal craft, the Americans had few means of opposing the ships of the Royal Navy. It is to their credit, however, that with almost a total absence of means of marine resistance they were able, time and again, to thwart the overwhelming seapower of Great Britain.

The Continental Army under Washington worked unceasingly in the spring and summer of 1776 to construct fortifications to protect New York City and the surrounding waterways against British attack. These defenses were situated, mainly, at the south end of Manhattan Island and on western Long Island, with another battery on the New Jersey shore of the Hudson at what is now Jersey City. These were to secure the waterways by the crossfire of heavy cannon. In June, the line of the Hudson was further protected when work was begun on the construction of Fort Washington on northern Manhattan Island.

(Fort Lee Visitor Center Display)

go, 15 miles an hour — the elevated, high-speed parkway is a relief.

Mile Mark 7.6 — Reach the exit to 125th Street. The high ground to the right, Harlem Heights, is where the Continental Army would regroup and set up defensive positions for the next encounter with the British, but they would also retreat from this position after the British made an end-around move to flank the American position from the northeast.

Mile Mark 8.0 — Look up the Hudson River for the George Washington Bridge. Just south of the bridge on the west bank of the Hudson is the escarpment on which Fort Lee is located.

Mile Mark 10.7 — Take Exit 14, Interstate 95 south and get into the left lane which goes to the upper level of the George Washington Bridge. On the bridge, move into the second lane from the right. Avoid the right lane that goes to the Palisades Parkway.

Mile Mark 12.6 — Watch for the exit to Fort Lee on the right. Take the exit and follow the signs to Fort Lee.

Mile Mark 12.8 — Circle back and watch for the entrance to Fort Lee on the right.

Mile Mark 13.2 — Follow the entrance road to the parking lot. Arrive at Fort Lee.

FORT LEE

Fort Lee, today, is a large 33-acre historic park that provides a historical experience as well as a breathtaking scenic experience. There are two overlooks that command spectacular views of the George Washington Bridge, the Hudson River, and the New York skyline.

Fort Lee

In mid-July 1776, General George Washington visited the site of Fort Lee and selected this position for a new fort from which the Hudson could be raked with cannon fire. The first fortifications were batteries built on this bluff, which was called "the mountain" opposite Fort Washington. For the better part of two months, it was an unnamed fortification which was called, variously, the post opposite Fort Washington, the post on the Jersey side, and the post at Burdett's (Burdette's) Ferry.

In September, the defenses were further extended when a square earthwork with four bastions was erected west of the bluff, on a site bounded by Parker Avenue and Cedar, English, and Federspiel Streets. In September, the post was christened Fort Constitution, and in October was renamed Fort Lee in honor of Major-General Charles Lee, second-in-command of the Continental Army.

It was Washington's hope that Fort Washington and Fort Lee would effectively block the Hudson to the ascent of British ships. In addition, a line of sunken ships and stone-filled timber cribs called cheveaux-de-frize was sunk in the river along a line now spanned by the George Washington Bridge to further block the waterway.

(Fort Lee Marker)

FORT LEE HISTORIC PARK

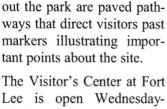

The views clearly demonstrate the strategic importance of Fort Lee. Throughout the park are paved pathways that direct visitors past markers illustrating important points about the site.

The Visitor's Center at Fort Lee is open Wednesday-Sunday, 10 a.m.-5 p.m., March-December. However, the grounds are open year-round from 8 a.m. to dusk.

A visit to the center is recommended. One of the highlights is an animated map that visually shows the entire

41

Mortar Battery

Mortar shells from this battery plummeted down in high soaring arcs upon the warships, tearing through the canvas sails and bursting upon the wooden deck.

This mortar battery, joined with heavy guns on both side of the river, made running the blockade a hazardous assignment for British sailing vessels.

It is believed this battery was used for mortars and consisted of four land mortars, a 13" brass, a 10" iron, a 10" brass and an 8" iron as well as one 13" iron sea mortar. Shells could be hurled accurately 1,200 to 1,500 yards — enough to provide a firing field reaching completely across to the opposite riverbank.

(Continued on page 43)

(Continued from page 42)

These mortars fired over parapets walls. No frontal ditches at this battery were necessary due to the virtually insurmountable cliffs on the east.

Firing Methods & Projectiles

Mortars were fired at an upward angle of 45° to 70° and were capable of hurling several different types of shells. Hollow balls filled with powder would explode on impact spreading fragments in all directions.

Incendiary shells, called "carcasses", were loaded with pitch or other combustible materials to spread fire when striking a target. Other projectiles, called "baskets" or "canisters", were filled with stones. All of these explosive and incendiary projectiles were called "boms".

Mortar crews were smaller than those manning cannons but the firing procedure was basically the same — sponging, loading, aiming and firing. However, as with all muzzle-loading pieces, crew teamwork, rhythm and weeks of practice were required.

(Fort Lee Marker)

campaign in New York City, including the Battle of Long Island, Harlem Heights, White Plains and Fort Washington.

Fort Lee found its place in American history during the 1776 British campaign to control New York City and the Hudson River.

After the siege of Boston, George Washington correctly predicted that the British would turn their atten-

Construction of Fort Lee

Fortifications were protected by obstacles, such as an abatis, or other major hindrances to assaulting troops. They were easily placed before a parapet, or breastwork, wherever trees were plentiful and were used to supplement defensive rampart walls or barricades.

Derived from the French word meaning a heap of material thrown together, the abatis was built of piles of trees or large branches sharpened to a point and turned toward the enemy's approach. They were entangled to form an impassable barrier for cavalry and infantry.

At Fort Lee, maps show that an abatis was placed to provide protection from an assault from the northwest exposure.

The use of an abatis either alone or together with other entanglements, let to an extensive tree-chopping program to supply longs for these obstructions and for battery to supply logs for these obstructions and for battery emplacements as well as to provide timber for huts and firewood for cooking and heating.

Bastion — Maps show that the fortification built on the high ground to the west was rectangular in shape with bastions at each corner. It undoubtedly was built to provide additional protection to the important batteries on the bluff and to prevent their capture by a land assault.

(Fort Lee Marker)

tion to New York City and the Hudson Valley. Along with the construction of fortifications at New York City and Long Island, Washington felt it imperative to build new fortifications along the Hudson River.

In July of 1776, work was begun on Fort Lee. On the opposite, New York shore, work had already begun on Fort Washington.

On July 12, Admiral Richard Howe sent two British naval vessels up the Hudson River. Cannon fire from Fort Washington had little effect on their passage. Washington then ordered that work on Fort Lee con-

tinue as quickly as possible. At Major General Israel Putnam's suggestion, sunken ships were placed in the river channel. With these obstructions and artillery fire from the sister forts, it was felt that no British ship could sail up the Hudson without sustaining severe losses.

King George III, after being stung by events in Boston, sent the largest force of British ships and troops that have ever been assembled by England for combat. By mid-August, Sir William Howe, British Commander-in-Chief, had brought to Staten Island an army of about 31,000 British, Hessian, and loyalist troops. Washington, on the other hand, could only amass about 19,000 troops to meet the challenge. Most were poorly trained and undisciplined state militias.

From August to October, the British and American forces were involved in battles at Long Island, Harlem Heights, and White Plains. The British then turned their forces against Fort Washington. On November 16, Fort Washington fell to an overwhelming assault by

---

November 16, 1776

After the Battle of Long Island, Washington removed the remnants of his army from Brooklyn, abandoned New York and withdrew to upper Manhattan Island, and in October moved into Westchester to fight the British. Behind him, he left a strong garrison at Fort Washington under command of Colonel Robert Magaw.

In mid-November Washington crossed the Hudson River near Peekskill and moved down into New Jersey, stationing himself both at Fort Lee and Hackensack. The British on the east shore then moved against Fort Washington. General Washington had wanted to abandon that post, but the final decision was left to General Nathaniel Greene, the commandant at Fort Lee. Instead of evacuating the Fort Washington garrison, Greene reinforced the post.

On November 16, the British attacked. The defending American garrison of 2,850 men faced a professional British and German army of nearly 15,000 men commanded by General William Howe. The American defense collapsed on all sides, and Magaw was forced to surrender.

Washington watched the battle from the summit of the Palisades at Fort Lee, but could do nothing to help the garrison.

(Visitor Center Display)

---

the British forces that captured about 2,000 American troops.

General Washington realized that with the loss of Fort Washington, Fort Lee was of little military value. He made preparations to evacuate his remaining army through New Jersey.

Washington at Fort Lee Watching the Battle of Fort Washington

From the summit of the Palisades, Washington and Greene watched in despair as the British overpowered the garrison of Fort Washington on the east shore of the Hudson. Hastily penciling a note to Colonel Robert Magaw, Washington promised to do all he could to withdraw the defending garrison to New Jersey if Magaw could hold out until nightfall.

He handed the note to Captain John Gooch, who was rowed across the river and delivered the message as the final determination was being made to surrender to the British. Gooch made a desperate return journey to his boat, dodging enemy bayonets and brought back word to Washington that Magaw had been forced to capitulate.

Nathanael Greene
by C.W. Peale

(Visitor Center Display)

An orderly retreat, however, was not in store for the Americans. On November 20, General Cornwallis ferried between 6,000 - 8,000 men across the Hudson north of Fort Lee. When word of the crossing reached

The British Invasion of New Jersey

The night of November 19-20, 1776, the British forces commanded by Lieutenant General Earl Cornwallis crossed the Hudson River and landed beneath the high Palisades about five miles north of Fort Lee.

This diorama depicts the landing and the difficult climb undertaken by the British to surprise the American forces.

It is based on the eyewitness watercolor by Davies.

(Visitor Center Display)

November 20, 1776

With Fort Washington in enemy hands, Fort Lee was useless to the Americans and plans were made to abandon the post. General Howe, in the meantime, made plans to cross the Hudson and move against the fort. On the night of November 19 two divisions of British troops commanded by Lieutenant-General Earl Cornwallis embarked in flatboats on the east shore, and at daybreak on November 20 landed at Lower Closter Landing (now Huyler's landing), about five mile north of Fort Lee. They were guided by John Aldington, a Bergen County loyalist. They climbed the Palisades and moved inland to take Fort Lee from the rear.

General Greene received word of the landing and abandoned the post. Washington also hurried over from Hackensack and personally directed the retreat to the Hackensack River. Cornwallis had to slow his march in order to bring up his cannon. Had he been able to move more rapidly the American garrison could have been trapped. As it was, Washington's soldiers barely managed to slip by the advancing British at an important road junction at Liberty Pole (now Englewood).

Cornwallis captured only a few Americans stragglers at the fort, but a large amount of stores and cannon fell into his hands. The American retreat had been so precipitate that the breakfast campfires were still burning when the British arrived.

(Visitor Center Display)

Site of the Landing of the British Army in New Jersey

The Hudson River dockside at Lower Closter Landing (now called Huyler's Landing) at the foot of the Palisades below Alpine, here Cornwallis' troops landed on November 20, 1776, in the invasion of New Jersey.

(Visitor Center Display)

Washington, he ordered an immediate retreat before his army was cut off and captured by the British. Most of the American supplies and artillery had to be left behind.

Newbridge Crossing

General Washington rode out from his Hackensack Headquarters on November 20, 1776 and led the fleeing American garrison from Fort Lee over the New Bridge. A large part of the Army was saved from entrapment on the Peninsula between the Hudson and Hackensack Rivers.

The old wooden span that carried them to safety was later dubbed "the bridge that saved a nation."

(Visitor Center Display)

FORT LEE TO ALPINE LANDING

Mile Mark 13.4 — Return to the entrance to Fort Lee and turn right on County Route 505 going north. Go straight through the lights and under Interstate 95 on Route 505.

Mile Mark 15.6 — Reach a stop sign. Go left about a tenth of a mile and turn right on US Route 9W North.

Mile Mark 16.7 — Pass CNBC on the left.

Mile Mark 21.3 — Watch for an intersection with signs to the Palisades Parkway Headquarters and the boat basin. Turn right at the intersection.

Mile Mark 21.7 — Pass the park headquarters on the left.

Mile Mark 22.5 — Reach a rotary. After yielding to traffic in the rotary, go a little over three quarters of the way around and bear right to the boat basin.

Mile Mark 22.9 — Reach the parking lot in front of the marina. Arrive at Alpine Landing.

Cornwallis' Headquarters

November 18, 1776

Restored with the assistance of the New Jersey State Federation of Women's Clubs by the Palisades Interstate Park Commission, 1933.

(Alpine Landing Marker)

ALPINE LANDING

Near the parking area is the Blackledge-Kearney House, believed at one-time to be the headquarters of General Cornwallis during the British landing and climb up the Palisades. Near the home is a marker about the trail taken by the British. Recent research, however, indicates that the landing likely occurred a day later and at a point further south than the markers indicate.

> Here began the Old Alpine Trail used by the British troops who first appeared in the State of New Jersey on the stormy night of November 18, 1776 in the unsuccessful effort of Cornwallis to intercept Washington on his way to Trenton.
>
> Placed by Polly Wyckoff Chapter Daughters of the American Revolution, A. D. 1928.
>
> (Alpine Landing Marker)

The park near the house is a very scenic spot along the Hudson. A walk out on the dock is recommended to see the steep cliffs to the west and to appreciate the difficult climb made by the British.

Notice

Cliffs and steep slopes are dangerous for your safety. Please observe park rules:

- Stay on designated trails
- Do not climb cliffs or slopes
- Alcoholic beverages are prohibited
- Trails close one hour after sunset

Violators will be prosecuted.

(Alpine Lookout Marker)

ALPINE LANDING TO TAPPAN

Mile Mark 22.9 — Depart Alpine Landing.

Mile Mark 23.5 — Return to rotary. After yielding to traffic in the rotary, take the first exit and climb back to the top of the Palisades.

Mile Mark 24.5 — Pass the headquarters building and bear right onto the Palisades Parkway heading north.

Mile Mark 26.4 — Bear right and take the road to the state lookout for a brief visit.

Mile Mark 27.1 — Reach the lookout. Park your car and walk to the edge of the Palisades to enjoy the view. The lookout also has a snack bar and gift shop — a great stop for coffee.

Mile Mark 27.8 — Return to the Palisades Parkway heading north.

Mile Mark 29.4 — Enter the State of New York.

Mile Mark 32.1 — Take exit 5S that takes you to Route 303 going south. There is also a sign indicating that this is the way to George Washington's Headquarters.

Mile Mark 32.8 — Turn right at the light onto King's Highway. There is also a directional sign for the Old '76 House.

Mile Mark 33.4 — Reach the stop sign just before the village green at the center of Tappan. Bear left at the stop sign and go between the village green and the Dutch church. Find a parking place for a brief walk around town. Arrive in Tappan.

Trial of André

The British spy, André, was found guilty in the Dutch church which stood, in 1780, on the side of this edifice.

State Education
Department 1932

(Reformed Church Marker)

TAPPAN

Village Church Green — On the green, a marker denotes the site of a former county courthouse. At one time you could find a Liberty Pole, stocks, whipping posts and a pound for stray cattle on the green.

The Courthouse

A log structure, with whipping posts and stocks, was erected on this Tappan green c. 1691. Here justice was administered to all of Orange County, which then included present Rockland. A more permanent courthouse and "gaol," built in 1739, was destroyed by fire in 1774. New City became the seat of government when the County of Rockland was set off from Orange in 1798.

The Orangetown Tricentennial Committee

(Village Green Marker)

"76 House"

Where Major John André, British spy, plotter with Arnold to deliver West Point, was confined before his execution.

('76 House Marker)

The Dutch church is the Reformed Church of Tappan and was organized in 1694. The present church was built in 1835 and is the third church at this site. The second church was the one in which the André trial was held as denoted by a marker on the side of the church. It was also a prison and a hospital in 1778.

Old '76 House — Just past the village green near the light at the center of town is the Old '76 House. The house was built in 1755 and didn't become a tavern until 1800. André was imprisoned here as denoted by the marker in the front.

DeWint House — The house is south of town and can be reached by car by turning onto the street just before the El Portico Restaurant. There is a marker on the right just after a bridge over a small stream.

DeWint House

Washington's headquarters, September 28 — October 2, 1780, during the trial of André, British spy, plotter with Benedict Arnold.

(DeWint House Marker)

The DeWint House is the oldest surviving structure in Rockland County and a good example of Colonial Dutch architecture. For over the last 60 years, The

Masons have maintained the house as a National Historic Site and a memorial to General Washington. The property is open to the public and free of charge, donations accepted.

The Carriage House, which is adjacent to the DeWint House, is the visitors center and contains many historical displays including a display about

---

Welcome to

George Washington's Headquarters

At Tappan

DeWint House — Circa 1700

Carriage House Museum — Circa 1850

National historic site owned and maintained by the Grand Lodge of Free and Accepted Masons, State of New York, Visitors Entrance, Open daily 10:00 AM to 4:00 PM.

(DeWint House Marker)

This house was occupied by

General George Washington

as army headquarters on four occasions during the Revolutionary War.

Here the general in 1780, after reviewing the evidence in the case of Major John André, Adjutant General of the British Army, approved the report of a board of general officers condemning André to suffer death as a spy.

Here, on the conclusion of peace in 1783, the British Commander-in-Chief, General Sir Guy Carleton, was "sumptuously" entertained by Washington, when they met to plan the orderly evacuation of New York City by his majesty's forces.

The house was built in the year 1700 by Daniel DeClark, leader of the Tappan Patentees, who bought all this part of the country from the native Indians in 1682.

The place passed into the possession of John DeWint, a wealthy planter from the West Indies, in 1746, and was known as the "DeWint Mansion" when the father of our country sojourned beneath its roof.

This historic site was purchased by members of the fraternity of free and accepted Masons of the state of New York and set apart as a permanent Masonic Shrine dedicated to the memory of George Washington in the 200th year after his birth, A.D. 1932.

Tablet erected in the bicentennial year by the Rockland County Society.

(DeWint House Marker)

Washington the Man, Washington the General, Washington the President and Washington the Mason.

The DeWint House was George Washington's temporary headquarters on four separate occasions.

1. From August 8 to 24, 1780, Washington stayed at the house while he was inspecting a redoubt on the Hudson.

2. Washington returned to the house on September 28, through October 7, 1780, for the trial and subsequent hanging of the British spy, Major John André. André had been captured after a meeting with American General, Benedict Arnold, at which they made plans to betray the fortifications at West Point.

3. Three years later - May 4 through 8, 1783, Washington and his key staff again headquartered at the DeWint House while negotiating the final withdrawal of British troops from New York City with British General, Sir Guy Carleton. Samuel Fraunces (owner of Fraunces Tavern in New York City) came up to prepare the dinner for Washington and his guest.

4. On November 11-14, 1783, the weather brought Washington to the DeWint house during a terrible snowstorm on his trip to visit West Point and later to New York City where he tendered his resignation. During the War he had forbidden his soldiers to play cards because it took time away from the pursuit of the war. Now, with the fighting over, a much more relaxed Washington took off his boots and played cards.

Washington, the Man

George Washington was born on February 22, 1732. He grew up to be a tall (6'-2") strong man and at the age of 17 he was appointed surveyor of Culpepper County, Virginia, the first public office he held.

On January 6, 1759, George Washington married Martha Dandridge Custis, a wealthy young widow. The Washington's had no children of their own, but they raised Martha's children from her previous marriage, Jackie and Patsy. The marriage began the relatively peaceful inter-war period in Washington's life, during which he farmed and served in the House of Burgesses.

On the morning of December 14, 1799, Washington awoke with an inflamed throat. His condition rapidly worsened. He was further weakened by medical treatment that included frequent bloodletting. He faced death calmly, as "the debt which we all must pay" and died at 11:30 that night.

Washington, the General

George Washington began his military career in November of 1752 when he was appointed adjutant of the southern district of Virginia and carried the rank of Major. Washington's desire was to gain a commission in the British army, however, the king's military advisors felt that officers in the regular British army were better qualified to lead troops against the French.

(Continued on page 66)

(Continued from page 65)

On June 15, 1775, the Continental Congress unanimously elected George Washington as General and Commander-in-Chief of its army. Washington took command of the army on July 3, 1775. His general order was on unity: "...it is hoped that all distinction of colonies be laid aside, so that one and the same spirit may animate the whole, and the only contest be, who shall render, on the great and trying occasion, the most essential service to the common cause in which we are all engaged."

Washington, the President

On April 30, 1789, 57-year-old George Washington took the oath of office as the first president of the United States. After Washington took the oath on the portico at Federal Hall in New York City, thousands of citizens cheered and 13 cannons fired a salute. Inside, Washington delivered his inaugural address in the Senate Chambers.

George Washington served two terms as President and was succeeded by John Adams, his Vice President. Washington was quoted "I walk on untrodden ground. There is scarcely any part of my conduct which may not hereafter be drawn in precedent."

The famous tribute by General Henry Lee, "first in war, first in peace and first in the hearts of his

(Continued on page 67)

(Continued from page 66)

countrymen," accurately describes the feelings of the American people for George Washington, today referred to simply as "Father of His Country."

Washington, the Mason

George Washington was initiated Entered Apprentice in the Lodge of Fredericksburg, Virginia in November 1752. He passed to the degree of Fellowcraft in March and was raised to the Sublime Degree of Master Mason in August of 1753. In 1788, Washington then served as the first Worshipful Master of what is now known as Alexandria-Washington Lodge.

Upon taking the oath of office for President of the United States, Washington added the Historic words "so help me God!" and reverently kissed the holy bible.

It is well known that Masonry has been closely associated with the history of our Nation. This was evident in 1793 when, wearing a Masonic Apron, presented to him by General Lafayette, and embroidered by Madame Lafayette, George Washington in a Masonic ceremony, laid the cornerstone of the United States Capital, at Washington, D.C.

(Visitor Center Exhibit)

Exit 15 to 9w
or Palisades Pkwy

TAPPAN TO STONY POINT

Mile Mark 33.9 — Return to the entrance of the DeWint House and turn right.

Mile Mark 34.3 — Go to the end of street that intersects with Route 303 just over the border with New Jersey. Turn left onto Route 303 going north and exit New Jersey once again.

Mile Mark 35.2 — Reach the light at King's Highway. Continue straight through the intersection and stay on Route 303 north crossing over the Palisades Parkway.

Mile Mark 40.1 — Go under the New York Thruway, Interstate 87.

Mile Mark 45.1 — Reach the intersection with Route 9W. Turn left and go north.

Mile Mark 46.6 — Cross over to the east side of a line of cliffs that guard the Hudson and head down to the river. Follow 9W along a ridge on the west bank of the Hudson River, which occasionally provides spectacular views of the river below.

Mile Mark 48.8 — Creep into the village of West Haverstraw in stop-and-go traffic.

Treason House

At Joshua Hett Smith's home, here Sept. 22, 1780, Benedict Arnold betrayed the plans of West Point to British spy Maj. André.

Historical Society,
Rockland County

(West Haverstraw Marker)

Mile Mark 49.6 — Watch for the Treason House marker on the left. Because of its location on the side of a hill just off a very busy Route 9W, you wonder if anyone has ever been able to read the marker.

Mile Mark 50.5 — Look for the memorial park on the left. The park is a tribute to veterans of the American Revolution, as well as America's other wars.

1779—1997

From the revolutionary soldiers led by General Anthony Wayne in the Battle of Stony Point and to all past wars, this cannon memorial is dedicated to all veterans living and deceased who have fought bravely to preserve our independence and everlasting freedom.

Battle of Stony Point
July 15-16, 1779
Charles R. Lewis VFW Post 8997
Stony Point, New York

(Stony Point Town Marker)

Mile Mark 51.0 — Watch for Dee's Country Deli on the left. The deli is a great place to grab a sandwich for lunch at one of several picnic areas at the Stony Point Battlefield, all with scenic views high over the Hudson.

Just past the deli on the right is the Pompey marker. Immediately after the marker is the turn-off to Stony Point. Make the turn

---

Pompey

An African-American was dispatched from this area by General Anthony Wayne to gain entrance to the Stony Point fort occupied by the British on the night of July 15-16, 1779. Under the guise of night trips to sell farm produce, Pompey had obtained the British password. He distracted the sentinels, enabling the Continental Army to storm and capture the fort. Pompey later served in the Orange County Militia.

Sponsored by the African-American Historic Society of Rockland County, established 1987.

(Stony Point Marker)

and proceed through a residential area that happens to be on the entryway to Stony Point.

Mile Mark 51.3 — Turn right at the entrance to Stony Point.

Mile Mark 52.7 — Arrive at the gate to Stony Point. After crossing the bridge, park in the parking lot and prepare for a healthy climb to the top of Stony Point.

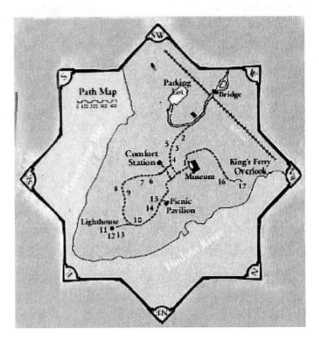

STONY POINT

One of the unique features of Stony Point is the historical detail presented by the many markers posted around the fort — and all this for an American victory

Stony Point Battlefield State Historic Site

On the night of July 15-16, 1779, Brigadier General Anthony Wayne of Pennsylvania led the American Light Infantry in a midnight assault against a British force that had occupied Stony Point. Approximately one hour later, the garrison had been captured by two American columns that had outflanked the front line defenses; the main assault column waded through the shallow waters of Haverstraw Bay on the south, while a secondary column approached around the north side of the Peninsula.

In 1826, Stony Point became the site of a lighthouse built to guide ships through the narrow passage of Haverstraw Bay at the southern end of the Hudson Highlands. The lighthouse survives as the oldest on the Hudson River, and was restored and relighted in 1995.

Today at Stony Point Battlefield State Historic Site, a museum with exhibits and an audiovisual program tell the story of the battle. Guided and self-guided tours, as well as musket and artillery demonstrations, 18th-century camp life activities, and numerous special events are scheduled throughout the visitor season.

(Stony Point Marker)

British War Veterans of America, Inc.

New York Branch of the British Legion erected this plaque to perpetuate the memories of the men of the 17th British Regiment of Foot who died near this spot defending the Stony Point Fortification against General Wayne's American Light Infantry on the night of July 15/16, 1779.

(Stony Point Marker)

that was achieved within the time frame of a single hour. Most of the markers are numbered and, for the most part, are chronological. There is a map that shows the location of each of the markers.

The American mission at Stony Point in July of 1779 was, no doubt, a dangerous one. George Washington sent General "Mad" Anthony Wayne and about 1,350 carefully selected soldiers to perform a night assault against the British stronghold at Stony Point. The garrison was held by about 700 well-armed, well-

This tablet is to commemorate the heroic capture of the fortress of Stony Point by troops of the Light Infantry under the command of Maj. Gen. "Mad" Anthony Wayne the night of July 15-16, 1779.

Erected by the Jewish War Veterans of America, Veterans of Foreign Wars of the U.S.A., Military order of the Purple Heart, American Legion of Rockland County, New York

November 11, 1980

(Stony Point Marker)

trained British soldiers equipped with heavy cannon. They were also well protected behind solid ramparts and two rows of attack-delaying, abatis at the base of the fort. The Americans attacked with no artillery support and no loaded weapons — just fixed-bayonets. Despite strength in numbers, the only real advantage the Americans had, was the element of surprise.

Although Wayne did not tell his soldiers, he regarded the mission as suicidal. In a letter, he left instructions for the care of his family and for his reputation after his death.

But the American Army of 1779 was a much different army than the one that retreated from New York City to New Jersey in 1776. Wayne's successful mission, which is well documented on the markers is a testament to the capability of this army.

Although Washington desperately wanted to use this army to oust the British from New York City, it was felt that the cost to do so would be much too high. But the army did possess the capability to sting the British with raids such as this.

Anthony Wayne
by E. Savage

At Stony Point, the Americans not only took over 500 prisoners, along with much needed supplies and armaments, but they also destroyed the fort on their way out. The British did rebuild Stony Point and temporarily put it back into service, but they eventually withdrew their forces,

The success at Stony Point, and the resultant threat that it created, helped to put the British into a defensive posture around New York City. It helped to turn their attention to an offensive campaign in the south — a campaign that would eventually lead to defeat at Yorktown.

One would think that the American success at Stony Point would have a prominent place in the history books, but it is often left out. Instead historians often turn their attention to the campaign the British mounted in the south and ignore the important events that also occurred during the same time-period in the north.

The Stony Point Battlefield is open Wednesday-Sunday during the day from spring to fall.

The British Occupy Stony Point

In late May 1779, a British force of more than 6000 men captured the promontory of Stony Point on the west side of the Hudson River and the small American fort at Verplanck's Point on the opposite shore. These strategic locations guarded the southern entrance to the Hudson Highlands. The British also took possession of King's Ferry, which crossed between these two peninsulas and gave the Americans a direct route between New England and the states to the south.

Having thus improved their access to a vital maritime highway — the Hudson River — the British were also in position to attack the American fortress at West Point only 12 miles north, but they had a more important objective. General Sir Henry Clinton had been directed to draw "Mr. Washington," the Continental Army, out of their winter quarters in Middlebrook, New Jersey, and into a "general and decisive action" that would end the rebellion. The British had already launched raids against the Connecticut coast in a vain attempt to lure Washington into battle and restore the King's rule to the rebellious colonies.

It was essential that the Americans take immediate actions to oppose both the British occupation of Stony Point and their presence in this vital military area.

(Stony Point Marker No. 1)

British Defenses: The Outer Works

After cutting down most of the trees at Stony Point to reduce cover for potential attackers and create a "field of fire" for artillery, the British constructed two sets of fortifications — the Outer Works, located near the present museum building — and the Upper Works, an unenclosed, incomplete fort located close to the river and comprised of earth and rock formations. Both works were situated on rugged terrain that afforded commanding views. The British navy also controlled the Hudson River, and protected the Stony Point peninsula. A small gunboat guarded the shallow waters of Haverstraw Bay in the south, while the HMS Vulture patrolled the deeper water on the northern flank.

A principal feature of the Outer Works was an abatis, a wall of trees that had been felled and placed side by side on the ground and pointed toward the west, or landward site, the most likely direction of attack. This barrier, one of two built at Stony Point by the British ran the width of the peninsula from north to south, and extended some 50 yards into the waters of Haverstraw Bay.

Artillery was positioned to defend the abatis, and troops of the 17th Regiment of Foot, as well as Grenadiers of the 71st Highland Regiment (Fraser's Highlanders), were deployed to protect the Outer Works and to repel invaders.

(Stony Point Marker No. 2)

The American Strategy

In reaction to Sir Henry Clinton's move against Stony Point, the Continental Army marched north from New Jersey, to protect West Point, and a plan was devised to counter the British advance.

Apprised of the formidable British defenses at Stony Point by Captain Allan McLane, an American officer who had gained entrance to the enemy fort, General Washington determined that a frontal attack in daylight would most likely fail. Consequently, a night assault, to be led by Brigadier General Anthony Wayne of Pennsylvania, was planned.

Wayne commanded the Corps of Light Infantry, a select force which probed enemy lines, fought skirmishes and executed difficult missions. Two columns — a total of 1150 men — would comprise the Continental force. The main assault group of 700 men, commanded personally by General Wayne, would wade through the waters on the southern flank. At the same time, a smaller secondary column would approach from the north. To eliminate the possibility of accidental gunfire and preserve the key element of surprise, both columns were armed with unloaded muskets and fixed bayonets. In the center of the peninsula, two companies of North Carolina troops, commanded by Major Hardy Muffee, would fire volleys to distract the British and divert the fort's defenders. An additional force of 300 men, under General Peter Muhlenberg of Pennsylvania, would be held in reserve. At midnight, July 15, 1779, the attack would begin.

(Stony Point Marker No. 3)

"I...imagined them to be British Troops, but found my mistake by being wounded and taken prisoner."

During the night of the attack, Captain Francis Tew was stationed near the abatis with four companies of the 17th Regiment, part of the total British garrison of 564 men. On this spot, a small defensive position called Fleche #2 had been constructed, and contained two Cohorn mortars — weapons which fired explosive shells in a high arc — to guard the approach to the Outer Works.

Stony Point was bounded on the west by a marsh that turned the peninsula into an island at high tide. At about midnight, an officer's picket — part of the group of 88 sentries on duty — heard the advancing Americans, fired warning shots, and then retreated. Lieutenant William Simpson, of Tew's company, described the events that followed:

About ten minutes later I heard a party of about 30 men in confusion on my right, and imagined them to be British Troops, but found my mistake by being wounded and taken prisoner. Soon after being made prisoner by this party, Lieutenant Colonel Johnson [the commander of Stony Point] came up, having from the extreme darkness of the night also mistaken them for our own people. He endeavored to give them some orders...to face the damned rascals!" They challenged him saying "Damn ye, who are you?" One or more of them I saw charge the Colonel with their Bayonets...the Colonel perceiving his error, narrowly escaped.

(Stony Point Marker No. 4)

"By the light occasioned by the flash of the gun I could perceive a body of them [the American Light Infantry] coming through the water upon the left."

Fleche #1 was situated on this hill, and mounted a brass 12-pounder cannon (one which fired a 12-pound ball) under the command of Lieutenant William Horndon, of the Royal Artillery. Horndon was unaware that the shots from Major Murfree's Light Infantry, who were firing in the center and approaching from the west were a diversion for the two other American columns advancing around both flanks. Lt. Horndon later described his experience at a British court-martial: *...I heard a great firing of musketry... and consequently opened with the twelve-pounder... By the light occasioned by the flash of the gun I could perceive a body of them [the American Light Infantry] coming through the water upon our left. I attempted to bring the gun to bear upon them, but could not effect it, the embrasure being confined.*

Meanwhile, a 3-pounder cannon located near the front of the present museum fired 69 rounds at the secondary column of Americans attacking around the north side of the peninsula, but it was too late to halt the Light Infantry's rapid advance. The main column—700 men wading through Haverstraw Bay on the south and let by Wayne himself—had already outflanked Horndon's 12-pounder, and was ascending the rocky slope toward the Upper Works.

(Stony Point Marker No. 5)

British Defenses: The Upper Works

The Upper Works was the main British defensive position. As in the Outer Works, an abatis spanned the width of the peninsula. Included in the abatis were artillery positions, but these weapons, mostly heavy ship guns, were intended for long-range, daytime targets and were kept unloaded at night when an attack was not considered likely. The guns were also extremely cumbersome. Brigadier General James Pattison described the difficulty of hauling cannon to the summit of Stony Point when the British were fortifying the peninsula: *"58 Men in Harness, besides many more shoving at the Wheels, were scarcely able to get up a heavy 12 [pounder]..."*

Four companies of the 17th Regiment and a detachment from the Loyal American Regiment were posted in the Upper Works, but the fortification was unfinished, being open on the east side toward the river. Scouts had informed the British commander, Lieutenant Colonel Henry Johnson, that Americans meant to attack Stony Point, and he eliminated passwords so no one could enter the fortifications at night. He also divided his forces in anticipation of a daytime assault. In the darkness and confusion of the battle, the men in the advanced posts could not retreat in time to defend the Upper Works. Had the upper fortifications been completed and the entire garrison posted there, the Light Infantry might have been repulsed.

(Stony Point Marker No. 6)

"... the enemy entered the upper work at the barrier at the same time I did."

Here, by the innermost abatis, a British eight-inch howitzer—an artillery weapon that could hurl a 46-pound explosive shell a distance of 1900 yards — was aimed towards the shallow waters of Haverstraw Bay to guard the southern flank of Stony Point. However, the main American assault column captured the weapon before it could be loaded or fired.

Lieutenant John Roberts of the Royal Artillery arrived at this battery just as it fell into American hands: *"...I concluded that the enemy were in possession of the Howitzer Battery and were pushing for the upper work, upon which I bent my steps that way but fell over a log of wood, and several people fell over me before I recovered myself. I have great reason to believe that the enemy entered the upper work at the barrier at the same time I did."*

These men were the vanguard of the American south column which had waded through the bay and around the outward abatis. Their advance might have been stopped by the small British gunboat assigned to protect the area, but it was absent from its post. The remainder of the column swept around the summit and approached the Upper Works from the rear. At approximately the same time, on the other side of Stony Point, the north column of Light Infantry was entering the inner abatis and meeting fierce resistance from its defenders.

(Stony Point Marker No. 7)

"For God's sake, why is the Artillery here not being made use of?"

In front of you is the Upper Works, and inside were two flank batteries, each with large shipguns. Lieutenant John Roberts of the Royal Artillery went to the left battery, nearest the bay, after the first shots of the attack were fired: Captain Clayton, seeing that I belonged to the Artillery, said *"For God's sake, why is the Artillery here not being made use of? The enemy are in the hollow and crossing the water!" I replied that the ammunition was not come up, and had it been...these guns...could not have been made use of.*

In fact, these heavy cannon could not have been lowered far enough to fire on the Light Infantry, who charged to the Upper Works with muskets unloaded, relying solely on their bayonets. In the pitch darkness, the American attackers wore white pieces of paper in their hats to distinguish themselves from the enemy in the ensuing hand-to-hand combat. Captain Henry Champion of Connecticut described his charge up the steep bank of Stony Point with the south column: The fire was very brisk from cannon and grapeshot and lagrange, as well as from small arms with ball and buckshot, through which our troops advanced with the greatest regularity and firmness without firing a gun or once breaking their order, except to climb the abatis and then forming instantly after passing them.

(Stony Point Marker No. 8)

"The fort and garrison, with Col. Johnson, are ours."

You are now inside the remains of the Upper Works. Within 15 minutes of each other, the two columns of American Light Infantry converged on the flanks of these fortifications. Lieutenant Colonel Francois de Fleury, a French engineer and professional soldier serving in the Continental Army, was the first man into the Upper Works, and, upon entering the Flagstaff Battery, struck the enemy colors. Later de Fleury became the only European to receive a medal from Congress during the Revolutionary War, awarded to him for his bravery at Stony Point.

"A little small arm firing and considerable bayoneting closed the scene exactly at one o'clock," wrote Captain Henry Champion. An hour later, at 2 A.M., General Wayne, who had been grazed in the head by a musket ball, wrote to General Washington: "The fort and garrison, with Col. Johnson, are ours. Our Officers and men behaved like men who are determined to be free."

Fifteen Americans and 20 British soldiers died in the battle. Among the dead was Captain Francis Tew of the British 17th Regiment, killed by musket fire after he had returned from the outer defenses in a vain attempt to rally his men. Only two officers, Lieutenant John Roberts of the Royal Artillery, and Captain Lawrence Robert Campbell of the 71st Highland Regiment, managed to escape to British ships offshore. The remainder of the garrison surrendered to the Americans.

(Stony Point Marker No. 9)

Opportunities Missed and Taken

"I was surprised when I viewed in the morning the difficulties our troops surmounted," wrote Captain Champion.

"This piece of ground was fortified by all British art and industry..." However, a night attack had undermined the effectiveness of most of these defenses, and high winds had prevented the British navy from coming to the aid of the embattled redcoats. Lightballs, or flares, had been prepared, and a signal rocket was on hand to call for reinforcements from the British garrison at Verplanck's Point on the other side of the Hudson; however, in the confusion of battle, they were never used.

The British had underestimated their enemy, whose abilities as professional soldiers had improved with each campaign. The Continental Army had carried out a well-coordinated night attack, assaulting a heavily fortified position. Except for the diversionary center column, they were armed only with unloaded muskets and fixed bayonets — ironically, just as the British had been when they attacked General Wayne's forces nearly two years earlier at Paoli, Pennsylvania, on the night of September 21, 1777.

(Stony Point Marker No. 10)

The Battle's Aftermath

Although Stony Point and Verplanck's Point became the focus of British strategy in 1779, they had shown interest in the Hudson Highlands before. On October 6, 1777, the British had landed here and attacked Forts Clinton and Montgomery, seven miles to the north, withdrawing two weeks later, after sailing up the Hudson River and burning the city of Kingston.

On May 30, 1779, the British returned. Six thousand troops left New York City, by land and water, and moved north toward Stony Point. The next day, while 40 American soldiers were finishing a blockhouse near where you are standing, the first British ships appeared in Haverstraw Bay. The soldiers burned the blockhouse and fled.

After the Battle of Stony Point, the Americans destroyed the fort, removed the prisoners, and captured supplies and equipment, including 16 pieces of artillery. Two days later, General Washington abandoned the peninsula, having determined that it could not be defended against the combined might of the British army and navy.

When the Americans withdrew, the British returned, and built a second fort with blockhouses surrounded by an abatis, but the war continued to expand; by 1779 Crown forces were fighting the French and the Spanish, now allied with the Americans. The additional burden on military resources and a lack of reinforcements compelled the British to abandon the forts at Stony Point and Verplanck's Point in October 1779. The American victory at Stony Point was the last major battle in the north. British efforts would now shift to the south, culminating with their defeat in 1781 at Yorktown, Virginia.

(Stony Point Marker No. 11)

"…with the greatest Intrepidity and coolness."

Near this location passed the north column of 300 American Light Infantry, commanded by Colonel Richard Butler of Pennsylvania. On the rocky height in front of you was the Flagstaff Battery, which mounted a 12-pounder cannon. This weapon, like many of the others in the Upper Works, was kept unloaded at night, and could not have been lowered enough to fire on infantry below.

Both Light Infantry columns were preceded by a select group of men known as a "forlorn hope," whose mission was to overcome sentries and remove barriers. It was a dangerous assignment; 17 of these 20 soldiers in the north column were either killed or wounded.

The advance party of Butler's contingent was led by Major John Steward of Maryland, who later wrote of another Light Infantryman: "…[he] conducted himself through the whole Assault with the greatest Intrepidity and coolness."

The description might well have applied to his own actions, since Steward, de Fleury, and Wayne were the only officers awarded medals by the Continental Congress for their courage and valor at the Battle of Stony Point.

(Stony Point Marker No. 14)

STONY POINT TO FORT MONTGOMERY

Mile Mark 52.7 — Return back to Park Road. Turn right on Park Road and follow it back to Route 9W.

Mile Mark 52.9 — Turn right onto Route 9W going north.

Mile Mark 55.9 — As you go north through the Highlands, the Hudson will begin to narrow but at this point it is very wide. Across the Hudson you can see the Atomic Power Plant that occasionally causes minor panic with radiation leaks.

At one time this area was full of Navy transport ships, docked here after World War II. Watch for the naval marker on the right.

Mile Mark 57.3 — As you come down the hill, watch for a peek through the trees of the Bear Mountain Bridge up ahead in the distance.

Mile Mark 60.0 — Reach a rotary and the intersection with US Route 6. US Route 6 crosses the Bear Mountain Bridge and makes a steep climb with many scenic views on the east side of the Hudson. Just before the toll gate to cross the river is a Fort Clinton marker. The area just south of the Toll Gate, including the Toll Gate itself, was the site of Fort Clinton.

Building a Fort

Early in the Revolutionary War, the Continental Congress realized that the Hudson River was critical to the American cause. If the British controlled the river, they could divide the rebellious colonies. Therefore, the Americans began work on Fort Montgomery in March 1776 and quickly erected several buildings. Sited where the river is narrow and currents made navigation difficult, the fort was

(Continued on page 92)

(Continued from page 91)

originally conceived as a large battery of cannons. At its heart was a "Grand Battery" of six 32-pounders commanding a long stretch of the river. As work progressed, however, it became clear that the fort could be attacked from the land. Therefore the earthworks were slowly extended to enclose the fort.

When the Americans discovered that the land on the opposite side of the Popolopen Creek was higher and would threaten Fort Montgomery if held by the enemy, they began constructing a second fort there, called Fort Clinton. They connected the two forts by a pontoon bridge. As labor was concentrated on the new fort, work on Fort Montgomery slowed. Other problems affected construction of the fort too. Supplies were often hard to obtain, morale was often low, and discipline was a chronic problem. Nevertheless, Forts Montgomery and Clinton were largely complete by October 1777, when the British attacked them.

(Fort Montgomery Marker)

Go halfway around the rotary and continue north on Route 9W.

Mile Mark 60.6 — Pass Fort Montgomery on the right and drive to a safe area for parking.

Mile Mark 60.8 — Watch for the Trading Post Restaurant on the right. There is a parking area for Fort Montgomery just past the restaurant on the right. After parking, make the scenic walk back to the fort.

Arrive at Fort Montgomery.

Burgoyne's Plan for 1777

For 1777, Lieutenant General John Burgoyne devised a plan to capture the Champlain Valley and the Hudson River. He would invade New York's northern frontier from Canada, while a smaller force invaded New York's frontier from the west. Burgoyne expected that General Sir William Howe would bring the British army occupying New York City up the Hudson River, and that the three forces would join in Albany. If Burgoyne's plan succeeded, New England would be isolated from the other colonies. However, none of the three forces ever reached Albany.

Burgoyne — Stopped by the Americans near Saratoga on September 19, 1777, Burgoyne received a coded message from Sir Henry Clinton and decided to await assistance. Clinton successfully captured Forts Montgomery and Clinton, but Burgoyne was defeated in a second battle near Saratoga on October 7, 1777, and surrendered his entire army ten days later. Most historians consider this the turning point of the Revolutionary War, because it helped convince France to openly enter the war on America's side early in 1778.

(Continued on page 94)

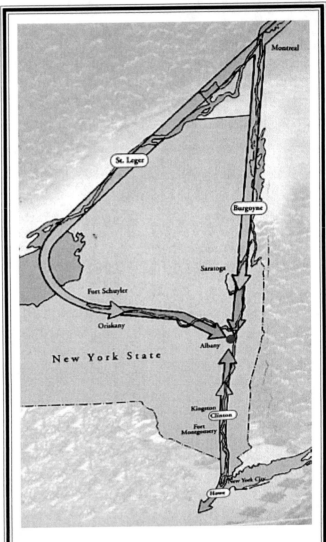

Montreal

St. Leger

Burgoyne

Saratoga

Fort Schuyler

Oriskany

Albany

New York State

Kingston
Clinton
Fort Montgomery

New York City

Howe

Howe — Burgoyne's plan for 1777 assumed that the commander of the British army in New York City, General Sir William Howe would cooperate

(Continued on page 95)

(Continued from page 94)

with him and move up the Hudson River. Howe instead followed his own plans to capture Philadelphia, leaving a large garrison to maintain control of New York City.

Clinton — Lieutenant General Sir Henry Clinton was left to command the British garrison in New York City after Howe moved to capture Philadelphia. Clinton wrote a coded message offering to provide a diversion in Burgoyne's favor, to which Burgoyne desperately responded he should do it "directly."

St. Leger — Lieutenant Colonel Barry St. Leger's force stalled at Fort Schuyler (the American name for Fort Stanwix in Rome). After the bloody battle of Oriskany and the defection of the Native American component of his expedition, reinforcements led by Major General Benedict Arnold forced St. Leger to retreat to Canada.

(Fort Montgomery Marker)

FORT MONTGOMERY

In the late summer and fall of 1777, Sir Henry Clinton, who was in command of the British Forces in New York City, was expected to move north and participate in a three prong attack on Albany: Burgoyne from the north, St. Leger from the west and Clinton from the south. However, Howe left the decision to move north up to Clinton's own discretion. His instructions were for Clinton to aid Burgoyne "if the circumstances warranted." Instead, Clinton decided not to move his forces against

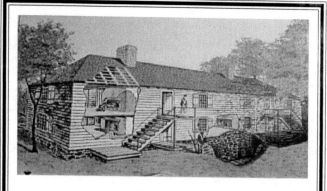

Barracks

You are looking at the foundation of a barracks built in the summer of 1776. This was probably a two-story building with a cellar under the northern half. Artifacts recovered from the site tell us a lot about the soldiers who lived here. In the 18th century, shoe buckles, brass and silver buttons, cuff links, glass tableware, tea services, and flatware were symbols of elevated social status. The large quantity of these items recovered from all of the barracks excavated at Fort Montgomery challenges traditional assumptions that these soldiers were poor and unsophisticated.

An abundance of cattle, pig, sheep, chicken, duck, pigeon, and fish bones was found in a large trash dump just outside the building's west wall, indicating that the soldiers were generally well-supplied with meat. The animals were probably butchered on site and the meat cooked in soups and stews that were eaten from bowls using large pewter spoons. The scarcity of bones and other debris inside the barracks suggests that the soldiers regularly cleaned the building.

(Fort Montgomery Marker)

Albany but to create a diversion that extended little further than Kingston, about 40 miles south of Albany.

In October, he moved up the east side of the Hudson and crossed to the west side at Stony Point. With a force of about 3,000, he moved north against the combined forces of about 600 Americans led by General George Clinton at Forts Clinton and Montgomery. The Americans held the forts until nightfall, but after losing almost half of their defenders, they withdrew.

Enlisted Men's & Officers' Barracks

The long foundation to the left was a barracks for enlisted men. The short foundation on the right housed the fort's senior officers and served as a commissary for storing food provisions. Items stored here were controlled and carefully guarded. Archeology suggests that only the northern half of the cellar was used for storage. The southern half of the cellar had a fireplace and may have been where the officers' servants lived.

Construction was virtually constant during the 18 months Fort Montgomery was occupied. The enlisted men's barracks was one of the first two buildings erected in the fort. It was followed by other buildings, gun platforms, earthworks, and the construction of Fort Clinton across the creek.

(Fort Montgomery Marker)

Today, the area where Fort Montgomery once stood has been cleared of brush and a walking path has been installed to tour the fort. There are several markers where the remains of the old fort have been uncovered.

It is difficult to see the strategic advantage of Fort Montgomery because most of the trees haven't been cleared from the area as they were in 1777. However, a walk across the two bridges north and south of the fort on Route 9W clearly shows the control the fort had over the Hudson below. The walk is recommended and the view is spectacular.

The Naval Battle of Fort Montgomery

When Sir Henry Clinton's British troops reached Forts Clinton and Montgomery on October 6, 1777, some of his ships began moving upriver to support them. First came two galleys, the *Dependence* and the *Crime*, which were rowed into position. Four American ships, the frigate *Montgomery*, the sloop *Camden*, and the galleys *Shark* and *Lady Washington* defended the giant iron chain the Americans had stretched across the river below Fort Montgomery. As the British galleys approached, a fierce cannon battle ensued. The *Dependence* fired 95 shots from its 24-pounders and many more from its smaller 6-pounders, striking Fort Clinton and the American ships. The American commander held his fire until his ship, the *Montgomery*, was struck. He then returned the fire and ordered the massive 32-pounder cannon on board the *Lady Washington* to do the same. The guns from both forts fired on the British galleys too.

(Continued on page 101)

(Continued from page 100)

Just before the battle reached its climax, two larger British ships, the brig *Diligent* and the sloop tender *Hotham*, and another galley, the *Spitfire*, came into view. Sir Henry Clinton later wrote that the sight of these ships "crowding all sail to support" the attack convinced him to begin his final assault. At dusk, the British drove the Americans from the forts, and the American vessels turned to support their fleeing soldiers. The *Montgomery* saved many Americans from capture by using its cannons to keep the British from encircling the fort. The *Shark*, the *Camden*, and the *Lady Washington* were ordered to rescue as many Americans as possible. As night fell, the ships tried to escape upriver, but the winds were not strong enough to overcome the ebb tide carrying them downriver. The *Camden* was run aground by its crew and was captured by the British. The *Montgomery* and the *Shark* were burned by their crews before they could fall into enemy hands. Only the *Lady Washington* escaped upriver.

(Fort Montgomery Marker)

The Battle of Fort Montgomery

To aid Lieutenant General John Burgoyne's British army stalled at Saratoga, Lieutenant General Sir Henry Clinton sailed from New York with 3,000 British, German, and Loyalist soldiers and flotilla of warships. On the morning of October 6, 1777, Clinton landed 2,100 of his men on the west side of the Hudson River near Stony Point. This force followed a narrow trail through the mountains, where they ran into a party of 30 men sent form Fort Clinton to detect the British advance. After beating the Americans back, Sir Henry Clinton sent 900 men around Bear Mountain to attack Fort Montgomery. The rest would wait to attack Fort Clinton until the first group had reach Fort Montgomery.

In the afternoon, the British began an assault on both forts, which were defended by no more than 700 men. At Fort Montgomery, the Americans kept the British at bay as the two sides exchanged musket fire. When the Americans refused to surrender, the

(Continued on page 103)

(Continued from page 102)

British stormed both forts. Taking advantage of the growing dark and smoky haze from the battle, many of the Americans escaped, but as many as 275 were taken as prisoners to New York City where they remained for much of the war.

Following the battle, the British destroyed Fort Montgomery garrisoned Fort Clinton, and burned New York's capital at Kingston. Then, receiving orders to join Sir William Howe's army near Philadelphia, Clinton's men destroyed Fort Clinton and sailed back down the Hudson. Although captured and destroyed, the forts had presented enough of an obstacle to keep the British forces in New York from aiding Burgoyne's army. The following year, in 1778, the Americans began rebuilding their defenses, this time at West Point.

(Fort Montgomery Marker)

Home of Isaac Garrison & Son, Revolutionary Cannoneers captured at the Battle of Fort Montgomery, 1777.

(Route 9W Marker)

FORT MONTGOMERY TO WEST POINT

Mile Mark 60.8 — Depart the Fort Montgomery parking lot and continue north on US Route 9W.

Mile Mark 61.3 — Look for a marker on the left in front of a home that was once owned by a Revolutionary War Veteran.

Mile Mark 61.9 — Detour from US Route 9W and bear right onto Old State Road. On the right in front of cemetery is a marker for the Benny Haven's Tavern, once a West Point Cadet watering hole.

Mile Mark 62.9 — Watch for the Captain Molly Margaret Corbin marker on the right.

Like many of the women and children who stayed with the American forces during the Revolutionary War, she was a "camp follower" assisting with cooking, cleaning

Captain Molly

Margaret Corbin, heroine of the Battle of Fort Washington, passed her last days on the former J. P. Morgan estate, near here.

Town of Highland Historical Society

(Highland Marker)

and nursing. She began her duties when her husband, John Corbin, joined the American army.

At Fort Washington, she went far beyond her normal duties and assisted her husband with a cannon after a gunner was killed by the British during Battle of New York City. After her husband was also killed, she continued to fire the cannon by herself until she was severely wounded. She was moved to the rear for first aid. After the Americans surrendered the fort, she was paroled to Fort Lee and later moved to safety in Philadelphia.

Molly Margaret Corbin was the first American women wounded on a Revolutionary War battlefield. She was also the first women to be awarded a pension by the United States for service to her country. She is buried at West Point.

Mile Mark 63.1 — Reach the intersection with Route 218. Bear right and follow the route into the town of Highland Falls.

Mile Mark 64.9 — On the right is a Freedom Road marker. This is a part of the route traveled by the 52 American hostages from Stewart Airport to West Point after their release from captivity in Iran, January 25th, 1981.

Mile Mark 64.5 — Watch for the West Point Visitor's Center and Museum on the right. Enter the parking lot.

Arrive at West Point.

WEST POINT

Visitor Center — The center is the first stop on a visit to West Point. It is open daily from 9 AM - 4:45 PM. It contains many exhibits including a large map that shows the history of the American Revolution. Also in

General George Washington

George Washington stands above all others as the conceptual founder of the Military Academy. He considered the site of West Point to be so strategic and significant during the American Revolution that he called it the key to the continent. Washington felt that if the British ever commanded the fortifications at West Point they would have a stranglehold on the colonies. He spent a significant portion of his tenure as Commander of the Continental Army at West Point and nearby Newburgh.

After the winning of our independence the new federal government acquired West Point in 1790. As President, Washington proposed a national military academy, and several Revolutionary War veterans advocated West Point as the site for such an institution. In his last official letter, written in 1798, Washington wrote that the establishment of a military academy was "an object of primary importance to this country." In 1802, under President Thomas Jefferson, the United States Military Academy was founded.

(Visitor Center Display)

the Visitor Center is a souvenir shop and an information center. Depending on the current US terror alert level, West Point may be closed for visitors or may only be visited by tour buses from the Visitor Center.

West Point Museum — The museum is behind the Visitors Center and is open daily from 10:30 AM - 4:15 PM. It contains one of oldest and largest diversified public collections of military artifacts in the Western Hemisphere. The museum is one of the departments of the United States Military Academy and supports cadet academic, military

and cultural instruction. Its collections cover all of US military history including many exhibits and displays from the American Revolution. The collection actually began with material brought here after the British defeat at Saratoga in 1777, twenty-five years before the founding of the military academy in 1802.

The first floor contains the "West Point" Gallery" and the "History of Warfare" Gallery. The "West Point" Gallery begins with the garrisoning of West Point during the Revolutionary War and chronicles the history of West Point and the academy. Exhibited artifacts include the sword of Polish patriot Thaddeus Kosciuszko, who engineered many of West Point's early fortifications.

The second floor contains the "History of U.S. Army" Gallery and "American Wars" Gallery. The "American Wars" Gallery is dedicated to the sacrifices of

---

West Point in the American Revolution

The history of West Pont in the American Revolution began in May 1775 when George Washington and other Americans recommended that the Hudson River be blocked to prevent the British from using the waterway to strike into the interior of New York or to divide the colonies in two. After a reconnaissance in June, the Americans decided to fortify the area near "the west point" of the Hudson River and Constitution Island.

From 1775 to 1776, American soldiers built fortifications on Constitution Island to block the difficult, double turn in the Hudson River. In 1776-1777, they concentrated on the new works near Bear Mountain, south of West Point, and installed the first iron chain across the river there. After the British destroyed these positions in 1777, the American leaders finally decided to fortify West Point. In January 1778, American soldiers began to build Fort Clinton, the first of a series of fortifications which soon made West Point the most important post in America. A key part of the West Point defensive zone was the great chain which was emplaced in April 1778 between Fort Clinton and Marine Battery on Constitution Island.

West Point remained an army post after the Revolutionary War. In 1802 the United States Military Academy was founded here among the remains of the fortification which made West Point "a key to the continent" from 1777 to 1788.

(West Point Marker)

American soldiers. Exhibits from the American Revolution include the British drum surrendered at Saratoga and George Washington's pistols.

Fort Clinton — At the top of the escarpment near the edge of the West Point Plain is a statue of Thaddeus Kosciuszko. The statue is at the place where a second Fort Clinton was located. There is a Fort Clinton marker in front of the stonewall, just below the Kosciuszko statue. The forts at West Point, which include Fort Clinton and Fort Putnam, were held by the Americans from 1778 to the end of the war in 1783.

The tribute to Kosciuszko at this position is appropriate since he was the person who engineered Fort Clinton. He built this fort at this "west point" along the Hudson and its strategic position is obvious. The fort clearly commands the river, overlooking the entire bend that the river makes around the point.

After 1778, the forts at West Point were the southern-most, defensive positions on the Hudson. They were considered very strong and they presented a considerable challenge to the British at New York City. The British were open to other ways of acquiring West Point other than an armed assault and it was Benedict Arnold that would offer one.

Fort Clinton

Originally named Fort Arnold, designed and begun by De La Madiere completed by Kosciusko, 1778-1780.

(West Point Marker)

In the spring of 1779, Benedict Arnold was commander of West Point but it is believed that Arnold was disenchanted with his superiors for their lack of appreciation of his service. He met secretly with the British and offered to sell West Point for 20,000 British pounds. The British were more than willing to negotiate. The matter was given such a high priority that British General Henry Clinton assigned his adjutant general, Colonel John André, to be in charge of the negotiations.

On the evening of June 19, 1779, Clinton held a banquet in New York City in anticipation of the conclusion of André's negotiations and the British acquisition of West Point. At the banquet, André was part of the entertainment, singing a British victory song.

Benedict Arnold
by H. B. Hall

Wars that Shaped the Nation

The Revolutionary War

In 1775, American minutemen at Lexington and Concord, Massachusetts, fired the "shots heard 'round the world." The colonists fought the British to establish their independence from northern New York to Georgia and from Massachusetts Bay to the Indian territories beyond the Appalachian Mountains. From 1776 to 1778, fighting centered near New York and Philadelphia. In 1780, the British focused on a campaign in the South. Unsuccessful and pursued by Generals Nathaniel Greene and George Washington, the British retreated to Yorktown, Virginia. In 1781, under the tightening siege of French and American forces, the British under Lord Cornwallis surrendered. The Continental Army moved to nearby New Windsor, New York until the British recognized American Independence with the Treaty of Paris in 1783.

West Point's role in the Revolution was critical. At the time of the Revolution, the Hudson River was a major transportation route in the colonies. The bend in the river here was the only major obstacle that a ship had to negotiate between New York City and Albany. The Americans recognized this at the outset of the war and began the first of a number of plans to fortify the ground on both sides of the river and construct a chain obstacle from West Point to Constitution Island. The British raided the island in 1777 as part of a campaign to take the entire river. In 1778, the Americans shifted to the higher ground

(Continued on page 113)

(Continued from page 112)

at West Point and its surrounding hills, building a fortress the British never challenged.

The weapons of the Revolution show the state of the gun maker's art at the end of the eighteenth century. All the guns were imported from Europe because America had no cannon foundries at the beginning of the war. Made of bronze, the guns ornate detailing characterizes the artistic nature of cannon casting in France and England. These smoothbore muzzleloaders could fire solid shot weighing 6 to 12 pounds. The shore weapon on the carriage is a howitzer, captured at Saratoga, that was designed to deliver plunging fire from a high angle onto entrenched troops.

(West Point Marker)

A few days later, André would change his tune when, by chance, he was challenged and captured by a small American patrol near Tarrytown, NY. When Arnold heard about the capture of André, he commandeered a barge and its crew. Leaving his wife and child behind, he ordered them to row him out to the British ship, "the Vulture" which was anchored out of range of West Point artillery.

George Washington just missed catching Arnold by a few hours after his departure. Washington was struck "very forcibly" by Arnold's conduct. When he found out about the full extent of Arnold's actions from incriminating papers carried by John André, Washington said: "Whom can we trust now?"

Constitution Island

In 1775, the first American patriots occupied Martelaer's Rock (across the river) and soon renamed it Constitution Island after the British Constitution. In 1775, the Americans built Roman's battery on the island — still visible at the river-line on the right. This was the first fortification in the West Point area. By the end of 1776, they also built Marine Battery, Hillcliff battery and Gravel Hill Battery. In 1777, the British destroyed these positions.

In 1778 and 1779, the Americans partially rebuilt Marine Battery, completely rebuilt Gravel Hill Battery, and constructed three interior redoubts to protect the river batteries from attack from the north. These fortifications added depth to the West Point defensive zone. Redoubt 7 is visible at the western tip of the island. Redoubt 6 can be seen in the winter on the high ground behind Romans' Battery.

(Continued on page 115)

(Continued from page 114)

In 1778, the great chain was anchored at Constitution Island in the cove below Marine Battery. The cove is visible to the right of Roman's Battery.

(West Point Marker)

Fort Clinton was originally called Fort Arnold, but for obvious reasons, the fort was renamed.

Trophy Point — Just north of the Kosciuszko statue is Trophy Point. The point is a collection of captured

Sherburne's Redoubt

In 1778, Colonel Henry Sherburne's regiment built a redoubt (a small enclosed work used to fortify hilltops, passes, etc.) in this general vicinity to cover the rear of Fort Clinton — the main fortification covering the great chain and the river approach. The redoubt also covered the western approaches to the west point plain and protected the northern approaches to Fort Putnam — the key defensive work against an overland attack. Remnants of Fort Clinton's parapets are visible on the eastern tip of the West Point Plain (to your right rear) and the restored Fort Putnam is visible on the hill to the southwest.

Sherburne's redoubt had to be constructed so that artillery fire from Fort Putnam could not fall into it. Originally the great chain was to be anchored below the redoubt. Little is known about the redoubt's construction. No traces exist today.

(West Point Marker)

Welcome to Trophy Point

The northern edge of The Plain at West Point has displayed captured enemy weapons since the Revolutionary War. In 1778, the Continental Army moved guns captured in the Battle of Saratoga in upstate New York down the Hudson to defend West Point. Washington's engineer and the designer of West Point's fortification, Thaddeus Kosciuszko, installed these guns in Fort Clinton at the east edge of The Plain and in the other works ringing the main forts. His statue is located at Fort Clinton, east of Trophy Point. By the end of the war, West Point contained the majority of the Army's heavy artillery pieces, some 160 guns.

At the end of the American Revolution, West Point became the principal repository of guns for the fledgling United States Army. Even before the founding of the Military Academy in 1802, West Point had taken on the additional role of educating officers in the sciences of engineering and gunnery. Captured ordinance naturally became a source of instruction for the cadets to learn how these weapons worked.

(Continued on page 117)

(Continued from page 116)

In 1837, the Military Academy's Board of Visitors formally recommended West Point as the Army's site for all trophies of the American Revolution and the War of 1812.

The cannon placed at this historic site are trophies of war. They have been captured, surrendered, and brought to West Point for display for over 200 years. As early as 1777, General Henry Knox ordered captured British cannon from the Battle of Saratoga to be brought to "West Point." Throughout the nineteenth century, other trophies and cannon were placed at this site and are now arranged and grouped by war.

These wars shaped the Nation. Beginning at east end of the display is the Revolutionary War area overlooking the Hudson River. Thirteen links of the "Great Chain" that stretched across the Hudson River to Constitution Island during the Revolutionary War is located here.

(West Point Marker)

artillery, including weapons from the Revolutionary War.

Near Trophy Point is an overlook that includes several historical markers. One can imagine the time that West Point Plebes (freshman) have spent at

The Declaration of Independence: Its Essence

...We hold these truths to be self-evident, that all men are created equal. That they are endowed by their Creator with certain unalienable rights. That among these are life, liberty, and the pursuit of happiness. That to secure these rights, governments are instituted among men, deriving their just powers from the consent of the governed. That whenever any form of government becomes destructive of these ends, it is right of the people to alter or abolish it, and to institute new government laying its foundations on such principles and organizing it powers in such form, as to them shall seem most likely to effect their safety and happiness.

We, therefore, the representatives of the United States of America, in general congress assembled, appealing to the Supreme Judge of the World for the rectitude of our intentions, do, in the name, and by authority of the good people of these colonies, solemnly publish and declare, that these united colonies are, and of right ought to be free and independent states; that they are absolved from all allegiance to the British Crown, and that all political connections between them and the state of Great Britain, is and ought to be totally dissolved; and that as free and independent states, they have full power to levy war, conclude peace, contract alliances, establish commerce, and do all other acts and things which independent states may of right do. And for the support of this declaration, with a firm reliance on the protections of Devine Providence, we mutually pledge to each other our lives, our fortunes and our sacred honor.

July 5, 1776

(West Point Marker)

French 6-Pounder Cast in 1761

Used by the American Artillery. Restored and mounted in memory of Brigadier General Henry M. Spengler, USA, 1913-1961, class of 1937, by members of his last command, 32nd Artillery Brigade.

(West Point Marker)

this overlook trying to memorize and absorb the historical facts in front of them.

The Great Chain

The Hudson River's narrow width and sharp turns at West Point created adverse sailing conditions and prompted construction of a great chain in 1778 as an obstacle to the movement of British ships north of this point. American soldiers positioned the chain to impede the progress of a ship should it attempt to turn into the east-west channel against frequently unfavorable winds and a strong current. Cannon were placed in forts and batteries on both sides of the river to destroy the ship as it slowed to a halt against the obstacle.

When finally completed, the 600-yard chain contained iron links two feet in length and weighing

(Continued on page 120)

(Continued from page 119)

114 pounds, including swivels, clevises, and anchors, the chain weighed 65 tons. For buoyancy, 40-foot logs were cut into 16-foot sections, waterproofed, and joined by fours into rafts fastened with 12-foot timbers. Short sections of chain (ten links and a clevis) were stapled across each raft. Later the chain sections were united.

On 30 April 1778, Captain Thomas Machin, the engineer responsible for assembling and installing the obstruction, eased the chain across the river, anchoring its northern end under the protection of Marine Battery in the cove to the right of the promontory to your front on constitution island, the southern end was secured in a small cove guarded by Chain Battery at the river's edge to your immediate right front. Both ends were anchored to log cribs filled with rocks. A system of pulleys, rollers, ropes, and mid-stream anchors adjusted the chain's tension to overcome the effects of river current and changing tide. Until 1783, the chain was removed each winter and reinstalled each spring to avoid destruction by ice. A log "boom" (resembling a ladder in construction) also spanned the river about 100 yards downstream to absorb the initial impact of a ship attempting to penetrate the barrier. Several links of the chain are located at trophy point to your left rear. A section of the boom was recovered from the river in 1855 and is now on display at Washington's headquarters museum in Newburgh.

The British fleet never approached West Point, and the strength of the great chain was never tested.

(West Point Marker)

Southwest of Trophy Point is a statue of George Washington on his horse. The statue is in front of the cadet quarters near the main parade ground and the West Point Plain. Its prominent position makes it very clear that West Point attributes its founding to George Washington.

Kosciuszko's Garden

Built in 1778 for rest and meditation by the brilliant Polish military engineer who redesigned and supervised construction of the forts at West Point making it the "Gibraltar of the Hudson" in the Revolution. This garden, reconstructed in 1968-69, is maintained by the generosity of the Polish American Veterans of Massachusetts and their friends.

May it ever be a place of repose in memory of the distinguished Pole who appreciated beauty and serenity even in the midst of strife.

(West Point Marker)

Kosciuszko's Garden — Just southeast of the statue and down a stairway between buildings is Kosciuszko's Garden. Kosciuszko, no doubt, appreciated the natural setting for his garden that was engineered by nature at this small ledge in the escarpment.

Fort Putnam — High in the northwest corner of West Point is the restored Fort Putnam. The fort was one of several small forts which were part of a defensive network around West Point. The fort affords a very strategic view of the river, Constitution Island and the West Point Plain.

Fort Putnam

Fort Putnam was one of many forts at West Point during the American Revolution. Built in 1778 by Colonel Rufus Putnam's 5th Massachusetts Regiment, it was the key fortification in the interlocking network of forts and redoubts making up West Point's defenses. From this site, the Plain and approaches to the Great Chain could be protected. Originally a wood and earthen redoubt, Fort Putnam evolved into a stone fortification which stands today after restoration during the American Revolution Bicentennial in the 1970s.

(Fort Putnam Marker)

Stony Lonesome

This rocky valley, named during the revolution, was a pass to the western defenses of West Point and was strongly guarded.

(West Point Marker)

WEST POINT TO NEW WINDSOR

Mile Mark 64.5 — Depart the West Point Visitor Center by reversing direction and heading back to the Freedom Road marker.

Mile Mark 64.9 — Just before the marker, turn right and head up the hill on Mountain Avenue, which is also Route 218 north.

Mile Mark 66.2 — Reach a stop sign near the intersection with Route 9W. Continue going straight onto US

Route 9W. Note the Stony Lonesome marker on the right.

Mile Mark 68.4 — Watch for the scenic overlook on the right. You can see West Point to the south-east, the Hudson River and Constitution Island to the east. The West Point Ski Area can be seen to the south.

Mile Mark 71.0 — Proceed down the other side of the mountain — watch your speed. It's very easy to coast over the speed limit, making the mountain road a likely place for speed traps.

Mile Mark 72.3 — Enter the town of Cornwall, home of the New York State Military Academy — West Point's unrelated younger sibling.

Mile Mark 75.1 — Watch for a flashing yellow light at the bottom of a hill. Turn left at the light onto Sloop Hill Road, County Route 74.

Mile Mark 75.9 — Watch for the Brewster Forge Marker and monument on the right. This forge was where the links in the Hudson River chain were made.

Brewster Forge Site

Parts of great chain designed to obstruct British navigation of Hudson, 1776-1778, fabricated here during the American Revolution.

Mem. Louis San Ciacomo, 1916-1980

(Forge Site Marker)

Mile Mark 76.4 — Pass Knox's Headquarters State Historic Site, the 1754 John Ellison House, on the left. For most of the 18th century and into the 19th century, the Ellison family milled flour on Silver Stream, which runs behind the house. The flour was shipped down the

Knox Headquarter

Home of John Ellison, erected 1754 by William Bull for Col. Thomas Ellison. Used various times between 1779-1783 by General's Knox, Greene and Gates during the Revolutionary War.

New Windsor Town Historian

(Knox Headquarters Marker)

Hudson River to New York City and the West Indies.

During the Revolutionary War, the house was used as quarters for Major General Henry Knox. Other high-ranking officers, such as Horatio Gates, were also quartered here. The home is open Sunday afternoons, June through Labor Day, and at other times by appointment.

Mile Mark 76.5 — Turn left at the light just past Knox's Headquarters and make the next right onto Old Temple Hill Road.

Mile Mark 77.3 — Follow Old Temple Hill Road across the intersection with Route 32 to the intersection with Route 300. Turn right heading north.

Mile Mark 78.1 — Reach the entrance to the New Windsor Cantonment. Just before turning right in the parking lot, note another Freedom Road marker on the left. This road is also part of the route traveled by the 52 American hostages from Stewart Airport to West Point. The Cantonment marker and the Freedom Road marker assert that Americans were able to celebrate their freedom along this road in both the 18th and 20th centuries.

Arrive at the New Windsor Cantonment and the National Purple Heart Hall of Honor.

NEW WINDSOR

New Windsor Cantonment — The New Windsor Cantonment is the last encampment made by General Washington's army before the end of the war. In October of 1782, a year after the American victory over

---

Welcome to
New Windsor Cantonment
State Historic Site.
The final winter encampment of the
Revolutionary War,
October 1782—June 1783.

A year after the American victory over the British at Yorktown, Virginia, in October 1781, General George Washington moved a large part of his army to New Windsor for winter quarters or a "cantonment." Here, some 7,000 troops, accompanied by about 500 women and children, built log huts for shelter, drilled and kept ready for a possible spring campaign, if peace negotiations in France where not successful.

At the same time, the army's grievances over long-promised pensions, land bounties and back pay threatened to erupt in rebellion. Fortunately, army discipline prevailed. Following the news of a provisional peace treaty, Washington issued cease-fire orders, effective April 19, 1783, bringing the eight year war to an end. The army was peacefully furloughed home.

Today, this state historic site preserves 120 acres of the original 1,600-acre cantonment. In season, interpreters in period dress demonstrate military and camplife activities.

(Cantonment Marker)

---

the British at Yorktown, Virginia, General George Washington moved his army to New Windsor for the winter. Some 500 women and children (camp-followers) accompanied his 7,000 troops. They transformed 1,600 acres of forests and meadows into a substantial military enclave or "cantonment." By late December 1782, they had erected nearly 600 log huts.

High-ranking officers, including Major General Horatio Gates, the commandant of the Cantonment, and Major General Henry Knox, Artillery Commander, were quartered in nearby private homes. Washington made his headquarters in the Jonathan Hasbrouck house (now Washington's Headquarters State Historic Site) six miles away in Newburgh.

Although the army was better housed, fed and clothed than any other time in the war, life at the Cantonment was still difficult. Peace negotiations

Troops on the March

Diorama

(Cantonment Exhibit)

in Paris progressed very slowly and there was concern that Congress still had not resolved issues relating to

Though he was active in the colonial militia before the Revolutionary War, Henry Knox learned artillery theory and practice from reading the latest treatises and manuals on artillery in his Boston bookstore.

Appointed commander of artillery in 1775, Knox tirelessly trained his gun crews. His efforts were so successful that even the British admitted after the Battle of Monmouth, New Jersey, in June 1778 that "no artillery could be better served" than the Continental Artillery.

Henry Knox
(Visitor Center Exhibit)

Portrait by Charles Wilson Peale, 1783, courtesy of the Independence National Historical Park Collections, Philadelphia.

(Visitor Center Exhibit)

the army's back pay, pensions, and land bounties. Rumors of mutiny rumbled through the ranks and threatened to ruin the cause of independence.

The problem reached a peak on March 15, 1783 when Washington was forced to confront the disgruntled soldiers at a meeting in the Cantonment's Temple Building. At this meeting he gave what is now known as the Newburgh Addresses. His speech was dramatic and effective.

Shortly afterward, there was long-awaited progress in the peace negotiations. Congress declared a

Continental Artillery

The Continental artillery in the early stages of the Revolution was composed of a number of volunteer units from different states. These militia units, including the Providence Train of Artillery, Boston's Ancient and Honorable Artillery Company, and others, were largely made up of men who had formerly served with the British in the French and Indian War.

At the outbreak of the War of Independence, American artillery was an accumulation of weapons of every type and size. Because of the difficulty in importing weapons, several foundries in Massachusetts, Connecticut, Pennsylvania, and New Jersey began casting iron and brass artillery to supplement those pieces captured from the British. Later in the war, the Americans received shipments of French artillery, usually of early vintage. Weapons of Dutch, Spanish and German origin were also used.

The first commander of American artillery was Col. Richard Gridley at the siege of Boston in 1775. Gridley was a veteran of the French and Indian War. He was succeeded by Col. Henry Knox, a Boston bookseller whose principal knowledge of artillery came from studying British manuals. Under his direction, however, American artillery was reorganized and molded into an effective arm of the Continental Army.

Four regiments of Continental artillery served in the Revolution. In addition to the Continental regiments, which were known by the names of their

(Continued on page 132)

(Continued from page 131)

commanding officers, numerous independent state and militia artillery units served the American cause. Continental Army artillerymen were paid more than infantrymen, probably due to the hazards of their duty, and the special training required.

(Visitor Center Exhibit)

"Proclamation of the Cessation of Hostilities" and enabled Washington to issue cease-fire orders, effective April 19, eight years to the day when the first

Artillery in Action

Units of the Continental artillery participated in most of the significant battles of the Revolution, beginning with the siege of Boston in 1775 and culminating with the heavy bombardment of the British at Yorktown in 1781. Artillery played an important role in battles such as Trenton, Princeton, Monmouth, Savannah and Charleston. Several American victories resulted in the capture of important stores of artillery: Fort Ticonderoga, 1775, Saratoga, 1777, and Stony Point, 1779.

(Visitor Center Exhibit)

The New Windsor Artillery Park
1780-1781

In November 1780, over 300 soldiers from the 2nd and 3rd Continental Artillery Regiments began constructing an artillery park in New Windsor, just north of the Hudson Highlands.

The park was a busy complex that winter: the men built their own huts, trained in artillery firing, and repaired equipment. Preparing for siege warfare, the artillerists trained intensively on ricochet-firing: the practice of firing exploding shells just behind an enemy's fortifications.

In late spring, the 3rd Artillery moved south to help protect West Point and the Highlands. The 2nd Artillery joined Washington's Army for the Yorktown, Virginia, campaign where they looked back with satisfaction at the training done at New Windsor. They could now drop exploding shells "just over the enemy's parapet, destroying them where they thought themselves most secure."

The New Windsor artillery huts were used as a military hospital for the remainder of the war.

(Visitor Center Exhibit)

shots rang out at Lexington and Concord. The army gradually disbanded, though still largely unpaid, and returned back to their homes or to new pursuits out west.

Today, at the New Windsor Cantonment State Historic Site, military drills and demonstrations, together with camp life activities, recall the critical months of the last encampment of Washington's Army of the North over 200 years ago.

The Figure of a
Heart in Purple Cloth

Headquarters, Newburgh, Aug. 7, 1782. The General, ever desirous to cherish a virtuous ambition in his soldiers, as well as to foster and encourage every species of Military merit, directs that "whenever any singularly meritorious action is performed, the author of it shall be permitted to wear on his facings, over his left breast, the figure of a heart in purple cloth, or silk, edged with narrow lace or binding. Not only instances of unusual gallantry, but also of extraordinary fidelity and essential service in any way shall meet with a due reward ... The road to glory in a patriot army and a free country is thus open to all," George Washington.

(Visitor Center Exhibit)

On the first floor of the Visitor Center, there is an exhibit on the Purple Heart. The Purple Heart Award was created by George Washington in a memo penned at his Headquarters in Newburgh in 1782. In 1944 the award was re-established to honor soldiers who were wounded in combat. In the future, the visitor center plans to have an exhibit that will list all recipients of the Purple Heart.

The Visitor Center also contains exhibits and an audio-visual show on the final chapter of the Revolutionary

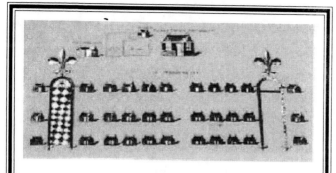

This detail shows the huts of the 7th Massachusetts Regiment as drawn by Private Tarbell, 1783. Tarbell identified his hut with his initials, "W. T." This illustration is from an 1890 copy of Tarbell's original drawing. Courtesy of Washington's Headquarters State Historic Site, Newburgh.

(Cantonment Marker)

War, when the Army of the North encamped at the New Windsor Cantonment from October 1782 to June 1783. The basement of the Visitor Center contains an artillery museum from the Revolutionary War.

In the encampment area there are exhibits including log working and shingle making as well as the Von Steuben camp, the regimental garden, the blacksmith shop, the Mountainville hut, a diorama of troops on the march and other exhibits. The parade ground is often used for musket and artillery demonstrations.

A City of Tents

The troops are allowed to put chimneys to their tents, and make themselves comfortable in them until their huts can be built.

General Orders

October 29, 1782

On first arriving at the cantonment in late October 1782, the northern Continental Army lived in tents until they completed building their log huts in late December.

The company encampment to your left recreates two lines of enlisted men's tents. Behind these were a line of company officers' tents, and then a line of regimental officers' tents This arrangement reflects the army's *Regulations for the Order and Discipline of the Troops of the United States*, written by General Baron Frederick von Steuben, based on the training he developed for the Continental Army at

V a l l e y   F o r g e, Pennsylvania, in 1778. Because of the terrain here at New Windsor, Quarter-master General C o l o n e l   T i m o t h y Pickering modified the plan by reducing the distance between tents.

(Cantonment Marker)

The Temple Building, a large building adjacent to the parade ground, is a reproduction of the original building that was constructed by the soldiers primarily for use as a chapel. It was here where Washington addressed his officers on March 15, 1783, to defuse a

A Matter of Amusement, The Regimental Garden

In General Orders, March 24, 1783, General Washington recommended the "troops to make regimental Gardens for the purpose of raising Greens and vegetables for their own use..." He hoped the gardens would contribute to their health and become "a matter of amusement" for them. The Quartermaster General was to advertise in local newspapers for seeds, and trustworthy soldiers were to be given passes to go out into the countryside to collect them. The next day, the 1st New York Regiment sent out a fatigue party of 1 subaltern, 1 sergeant, 1 corporal and 36 privates, equipped with axes, to begin work on their regiment's garden.

There is no record of how the gardens fared during the few remaining months before the troops were furloughed home by mid-June. Nor is it known what vegetables were planted. The vegetables grown here are "heirloom" vegetables, representing — as much as possible — varieties available in the late 18th century in this area.

(Cantonment Marker)

The Temple or New Building

In December 1782, at the suggestion of the Reverend Israel Evans, chaplain to the New Hampshire regiments, General Washington ordered the troops to construct a large building that would serve as a chapel for Sunday services. The resulting Temple of Virtue, as it was known — also called the New Building and Public Building — was 110 feet by 30 feet. It was used also for courts-martial hearings, commissary and quartermaster activities and officers' functions.

On March 15, 1783, an officers' challenge to General Washington and Congress, now known as the Newburgh Addresses, was countered by Washington at a dramatic meeting held in the Temple Building. A month later, news of the provisional peace treaty and Congress's "Proclamation of the Cessation of Hostilities" enabled Washington to issue cease-fire orders. A copy of the proclamation was posted on the door of the Temple Building. In June 1783, the troops were furloughed home.

The original Temple Building was damaged by lightening in June 1783, and was sold when the army auctioned off many of the huts and surplus equipment. Today's structure is a representation built in 1964-1965.

(Cantonment Marker)

possible mutiny. Behind the temple is a tall stone monument placed in memory of the Masons who served here, including George Washington himself.

The cantonment is open to the public from Mid-April through Oct., Wed.-Sat. 10 AM - 5 PM, Sun. 1-5 PM.

Winter of Discontent

Although many officers were allowed to leave the army on furlough for the winter, among those remaining there was considerable unrest caused by the failure of Congress to fulfill promises of back pay and pensions. Anonymous letters circulated among the officers in camp suggesting that the army refuse to be disbanded if peace came before the promises were kept.

Fearing that the unrest among his officers might become an open revolt, Washington summoned them to a meeting in the Temple of Virtue on March 15, 1783. In a dramatic address, he eloquently defused any possible defiance of Congress, and convinced his subordinates to have faith in the government.

(Cantonment Marker)

The Temple Hill Monument

This monument commemorates the Continental Army's final encampment and the events associated with it. It was erected in 1891 near the site of the Temple Building, where General Washington addressed his officers in response to the Newburgh Addresses of March 15, 1783. The winter view (when the trees have lost their foliage) encompasses the area where the 1st and 3rd Massachusetts Brigades encamped—186 huts—approximately parallel to present-day Route 300. In the distance beyond the slope of a ridge, near today's I-87, New York, New Jersey, New Hampshire and Maryland troops were encamped—251 huts. A causeway, an elevated road about 1,400 feet long, was built through a swampy area to connect the two lines of troops.

The third concentration of troops, the 2nd Massachusetts Brigade—127 huts—was located one-half mile east of Temple Hill near today's Route 32.

This tablet is inserted by the Masonic Fraternity of Newburgh in memorial of — Washington — and his Masonic compeers under whose direction and plans the temple was constructed and in which communications of the fraternity were held — 1783.

(Cantonment Marker)

"Disbanding of the Continental Army," by H.A. Ogden was published in *Harper's Weekly* in 1883, commemorating the centennial of the end of the Revolutionary War.

(Cantonment Marker)

The Mountainville Hut

After the Continental Army troops left the cantonment in June 1783, the Quartermaster Department began selling buildings and equipment for which it had no further use. According to local tradition, Nathaniel Sackett, an area merchant, purchased one or more of the huts. He took them to his property at nearby Mountainville, near Cornwall, where they became a wing of a private dwelling. "Rediscovered" in 1933, the structure was dismantled and reassembled here at Temple Hill.

(Cantonment Marker)

NEW WINDSOR TO NEWBURGH

Mile Mark 78.1 — Depart the New Windsor Cantonment heading south on Route 300.

Mile Mark 79.6 — Reach a five-corner intersection. Make an immediate right onto Route 94 going west.

Mile Mark 79.8 — Watch for the Edmonston House just up on the right. Turn into the parking lot at the house. There is a marker in front of the house.

142

Like the Ellison House (Knox's Headquarters), the Edmonston House was also used to quarter officers while the American army was encamped nearby at the New Windsor Cantonment.

From the Edmonston house, one can see and hear the New York Thruway just a short distance away. The thruway actually passes through part of the original cantonment where New York, New Jersey, New Hampshire and Maryland troops were encamped.

With our country's history so close to the thruway, one wonders why there are no historical signs on it. They have signs for every route, town, restaurant, motel and gas station off the thruway, but few for the very important historical attractions that are just off the highway.

From the entrance to the Edmonston House, turn left onto Route 94 going east through the five-corner intersection.

Mile Mark 81.7 — Watch for a split in the road. Bear left at the split.

Mile Mark 83.4 — Turn left onto Route 9W north.

Mile Mark 84.2 — Watch for a little park on the left and the light at the intersection with Washington Street (appropriately named). Turn right and proceed down Washington Street and pass through a neighborhood that has clearly known better days.

Mile Mark 84.8 — After passing several intersections, you will come to a light at the intersection with Liberty Street (also appropriately named). George Washington's Headquarters is in the fenced park on the southeast corner of this intersection. Turn right at the intersection.

Mile Mark 85.0 — Proceed down Liberty Street and look for a small house that was once George Washington's Headquarters on the left. If parking is available in front of the park, turn around and park on the street. If not, go to the end of the fence and turn left into the visitor parking area.

Arrive at Washington's Headquarters at Newburgh.

NEWBURGH

George Washington and his wife, officers, slaves, and servants lived and worked in this fieldstone farmhouse from April 1782 to August 1783. The home was well situated with protection from the Hudson on the east, the forts at West Point to the south and the cantonment at New Windsor to the west.

The house, the residence of Jonathan Hasbrouck, was made Washington's last military headquarters while America awaited the Paris peace treaty. Out of all the

homes that Washington called headquarters, this one was his for the longest time period of any during the war — 18 months. For 12 of these months, his wife Martha lived here also.

During this time, Washington maintained a strong army while planning to disband it. He negotiated with contentious individuals in the Congress and elsewhere and dealt with problems of supply, training, pay and morale affecting his troops. He rejected a suggestion of an American monarchy, defused a potential mutiny among his officers, and proffered advice on the future of the new republic.

The Hasbrouck property, acquired and opened by the State of New York in 1850, was the first publicly operated historic site in the United States. The Hasbrouck House is furnished to reflect Washington's 18-month stay and is open for guided tours.

As part of the centennial celebration of the end of the American Revolution, an imposing limestone monument was constructed at Newburgh. Above the gates and arches of this "Tower of Victory" are bronze statues of soldiers and officers of the Continental Army, while a life-size statue of Washington is at its center.

There is a scenic view of the Hudson River from the area near the Stone Monument. To the south, you can see the Highlands in the distance with the very strategic crack in the mountains where the river squeezes by West Point.

The Hasbrouck House is open mid-April through Oct., Wed.-Sat. 10 AM - 5 PM and Sun. 1-5 PM. It is also open in February for a three-day celebration of Washington's Birthday over Presidents' weekend.

NEWBURGH TO KINGSTON

Mile Mark 85.0 — Depart Washington's Headquarters. Go back to the light at the intersection with Washington Street and turn left.

Mile Mark 85.8 — Watch for the light at the intersection with Route 9W — look for the park in the southwest corner of the intersection. Turn right onto Robinson Avenue, which is Route 9W going north.

Mile Mark 86.0 — Cross the intersection with Broadway. Broadway is the main thoroughfare through Newburgh and has been undergoing much needed renovation.

Mile Mark 86.2 — Pass Downing Park on the right.

Mile Mark 87.1 — Reach the intersection with I84.

On a longer visit to the area, it is recommended that you go east on I84, re-cross the Hudson River and visit Fishkill. After crossing the Hudson and just off the first exit (take 9D north) is the Mount Gulian Ver Plank Homestead. This circa 1730 Dutch Colonial homestead overlooking the

Verplanck House

Built 1740, by Gulian Verplanck. Burned 1931. Headquarters Baron Steuben, 1782. Society of Cincinnati organized here in 1783.

(Fishkill Marker)

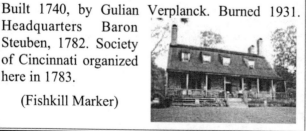

Hudson was the headquarters of General von Steuben during the final days of the Revolution.

Just to the south of the next exit off I84 on US Route 9 and on the left is the Van Wyck Homestead Museum. This restored Dutch colonial housed officers of Washington's army. It was also the army's northern supply depot headquarters and is reputedly the setting for James Fennimore Cooper's The Spy. It contains

Fishkill Encampment

1776-1783

In adjoining fields, barracks were built by General Gates under orders of George Washington to accommodate an encampment of over 2000 soldiers. The Van Wyck home served as army headquarters for General Gates, General Putnam and Colonel Hay. Frequent meetings were held here by La Fayette, Von Steuben, John Jay, Alexander Hamilton and other patriots.

(Fishkill Marker)

portraits by Ammi Phillips as well as artifacts from the Fishkill Depot and Barracks.

About a mile to the north on US Route 9 is the intersection with Fishkill's main street. Two historic churches are near the intersection. The Trinity

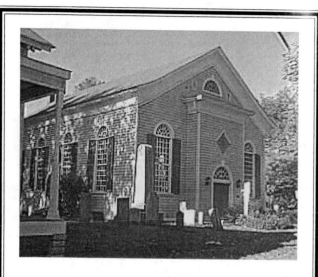

✝

Trinity Church

Organized in communion with the Church of England by the Rev. Samuel Seabury, 1756. The first rector Rev. John Beardsley, Oct. 26, 1766. Reincorporated, Oct. 13, 1785 and Oct. 16, 1796. This building was erected about 1769. Occupied by the New York Provincial Convention which removed from White Plains, Sept. 3, 1776. Used for a military hospital by the army of General Washington until disbanded, June 2, 1783. Pro Deo et Patria, 1756 — 1894.

(Fishkill Marker)

Dutch Church

Reformed church of Fishkill, organized 1716, built 1725 occupied 1776 by New York Provincial Congress, also a prison during Revolution.

(Fishkill Marker)

Episcopal Church served as a military hospital during the Revolutionary War. The Dutch Reformed Church housed prisoners of war.

Mile Mark 87.1 — Back on the west side of the Hudson River, continue north on US Route 9W.

Mile Mark 92.3 — Watch for the Gomez Mill House marker on the right. Turn right onto Mill House Road.

Mile Mark 92.4 — Turn left into the driveway and park in the parking lot for a visit to the mill house.

The Gomez Mill House is the oldest extant Jewish home in North America. It was founded about 1714 as a fur trading post by Luis Moses Gomez, a Sephardic

Gomez Mill House

On property that once served as an Indian ceremonial ground, the Gomez Mill House, built in 1714 by Lewis Moses Gomez, was continuously occupied for more than 280 years. It was sold to Wolfert Acker before the Revolutionary War, then to William Henry Armstrong, who occupied it for five decades. Dard Hunter, the famous paper maker, also lived here and ended up building a mill. Then, after W.W.II, the Starin family owned it until 1984, when the Gomez Historical Society decided to start restoration.

History compiled by Bethany Johnston, Troop 357, GSA

(Mill House Marker)

Jew. Gomez later turned it into a very successful mill operation and eventually became one of the richest men in New York.

In 1772, the home was sold to Wolfert Acker, who supported the Patriot's cause. Many meetings were held at the Mill House by the militia. Acker, a Christian of Dutch ancestry, would read inspirational passages from "his family Bible box" to his guests.

Today, the house and mill area have been restored and are open to visitors.

Mile Mark 92.6 — Return back to Route 9W. Turn right heading north.

Mile Mark 101.2 — Reach the intersection with US Route 44. To the east on the opposite side of the river is the city of Poughkeepsie, which also has Revolutionary War era sites including the Clinton House, circa 1765 (549 Main Street), and the Glebe House, circa 1767 (635 Main Street). The Glebe House was home to Rev. John Beardsley of Trinity Church in Fishkill and

Christ Church in Poughkeepsie. Beardsley was exiled to Canada during the Revolution for his loyalist sympathies.

To the north of Poughkeepsie and also recommended on a longer visit to the area are three national historic sites: the home of Franklin Delano Roosevelt, the home of Eleanor Roosevelt (Val-Kill) and the Vanderbilt Mansion.

Mile Mark 103.7 — Reach the intersection with Route 299 to New Paltz. New Paltz is the home of a historic landmark that predates the American Revolution and is another recommended site on a longer visit to the area. Huguenot Street, "the oldest street in America", has several stone homes built during the 18th century and one built during the 17th century (1692). All the homes remain in their original locations and are fully furnished with period pieces.

Nearby is the Mohonk Mountain House. The house is a castle-like, resort hotel that offers spectacular views and hiking trails. Visitors do not have to stay there to use the facilities — day-passes are available.

Mile Mark 105.9 — Begin a drive through a part of US Route 9W that has been set aside for God. You will pass Cabrini on the Hudson, Santa Maria, Congregation of the Christian Brothers, Holy Cross Monastery (with a gift shop), Church of the Ascension, Marist Brothers, Mount Saint Alphonsus, the Mount and Mother of Perpetual Health Monastery.

Mark 111.4 — Pass the Headless Horseman Hayride and Haunted House, home of the "best haunted hayride in the country".

Mile Mark 115.3 — Pass through the town of Esopus.

Mile Mark 116.3 — Cross the bridge over Rondout Creek. If you can safely pull over and park, there are scenic overlooks from the bridge. To the east, the creek enters the Hudson River. To

the west, a suspension bridge crosses Rondout creek. The Rondout harbor can be seen directly below each side of the bridge.

Mile Mark 116.6 — After the bridge, watch for an upcoming left turn. Make the turn onto Garraghan Drive.

Mile Mark 116.7 — Turn left on Broadway and proceed down to the Rondout Harbor.

In October of 1777, local militia fired upon a British ship that had entered

Rondout creek and was heading for Rondout Harbor. The British landed and quickly crushed the resistance. From the harbor, they marched west to the Kingston Stockade.

The harbor is a great place to visit. Among the attractions are the Visitor Center, the Maritime Museum and the Rip Van Winkle Cruise Ship.

Mile Mark 116.9 — Reverse direction and go west on Broadway toward the Kingston Stockade.

Mile Mark 117.4 — Bear right at the light and continue west on Broadway.

Mile Mark 117.9 — Reach the intersection with Brewster Street, an old Irish neighborhood. Watch for the old Kingston Library and High School coming up on the left. City Hall is coming up on the right.

Mile Mark 118.9 — As you approach the intersection with Albany Avenue, get into the left lane. Turn left at the intersection.

Mile Mark 119.0 — Pass a park on the left with statues of Hudson, Stuyvesant and Clinton. Get into the right lane and turn right onto Clinton Avenue.

Mile Mark 119.2 — Go past Main Street. Watch for the Visitor Center, a white building, on the right.

Mile Mark 119.3 — Turn into the parking lot just after the center or find a metered space on the opposite side of the street near Main Street.

Arrive at the Kingston Stockade.

KINGSTON

On October 16, 1777, British troops invaded Kingston
and torched over 300 homes, barns and other buildings.
At the time, Kingston was the capital of New York,
which was forced out of New York City when the
British invaded there. The invasion forced the state
government to move even further north and would
eventually settle at Albany.

British Major General John Vaughan, who led the
invasion, justified the destruction of the city because it
was "a nursery for almost every villain in the country."
But many of the stone houses in Kingston's stockade
still stand. Today, these homes, despite the torching,
are used as residences, offices and restaurants, a
testament to their sturdiness over the centuries.

From the Visitor's Center, begin a walk around the
stockade on Clinton Avenue to the first of the surviving
houses, the 1676 Senate House at 331 Clinton Ave.
Built in 1676, it is the oldest public building in
America. Descendants of the original builder, Wessel
Ten Broeck, occupied the residence until they deeded it
to New York State in 1888.

The first New York State Senate met here in September
and October of 1777 when the building was the home

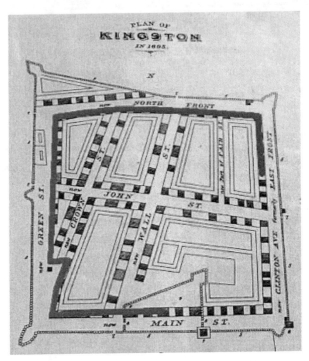

of Abraham Van Gaasbeek. They met to form a new state government. They adopted a system, comprising a senate, assembly, governor, and judiciary that still exist today. Every one of the assembled delegates

Senate House

Col. Wessel Ten Broeck born at Westphalia, 1635. Erected this stone house about 1676 wherein the first senate of State of New York met after the adoption of the first constitution 1777, until the burning of Kingston, October 16, 1777.

(Kingston Marker)

> As a memorial to those heroic citizens of
>
> ## Kingston
>
> Because of whose patriotism the village was burned by the British forces under the command of Maj. Gen. John Vaughan on the 16th day of October 1777.
>
> This tablet is erected by one of the members of Wiltwyck Chapter Daughters of the American Revolution on the 16th day of October 1914.
>
> (Kingston Marker)

placed their lives and property at risk by being so openly disloyal to the Crown.

The Senate House is open Wednesdays to Saturdays from 10 AM - 5 PM and Sundays from 1-5 PM from April-December. In March it is open only on weekends. Tours are offered periodically.

Walk north to the intersection with North Front Street, turn left and walk to the intersection with Crown Street. In the southeast corner of the intersection is Peace Park. This is the site where the Jacobus S. Bruyn House once stood. Bruyn was a company commander during the Revolution who was captured in 1777 and held prisoner until the end of the war.

Walk west to the Hoffman House Tavern that is just before the intersection with Greene Street. The tavern is a great place for food and spirits and is a recommended spot to return to later for dinner. The house is situated in the northwest corner of the stockade. The original house built prior to 1658 was much smaller than the current building. Musket holes in the upper floor indicate that the original house was likely used as a corner defensive position for the

Hoffman House

Built by Nicholas Hoffman 1711 on part of Crown Grant of land made to his father Martinus in 1688. This is the northwest corner of the old stockade.

Friends of the Senate House, 1965.

(Kingston Marker)

stockade. Anthony Hoffman, a member of the Provincial Congress and a signer of the Article of Confederation, lived in the house during the mid-1770's.

Turn south on Green Street. Watch for the intersection with Lucas Street on the right. Just pass this intersection, also on the right is the Egbert Dumond

The Stockade

The first European settler came here between 1652 and 1653 to farm the rich land in the lowlands along the Esopus Creek near the fields where native Americans had grown maize for centuries. Friction between the settlers and the Esopus Indians over trespassing on each other's land began almost immediately and grew to acts of assaults on both. In May of 1658, the settlers appealed for help to Peter Stuyvesant, director-general of the New Netherlands

(Continued on page 161)

(Continued from page 160)

Colony. Stuyvesant ordered the settlers to move to a central location guarded by a stockade. He selected the bluff above the flats because its height afforded a natural defense on three sides: North (North Front Street), west (Green Street) and east (Clinton Avenue). Stuyvesant told the Esopus Indians they should sell the land for the stockade area, but they gave it as gift instead.

The Stockade was built in three weeks and stood 14 feet high. Between 60 and 70 settlers took their wood houses and barns down and rebuilt them within the Stockade area. They called the walled village Wiltwyck. Gates gave the men access to their fields, but women and children were confined to life within the 1,200 by 1,300 foot perimeter of the wall. The original portion (c. 1660) of the Hoffman House stood in the northwest area of the Stockade, and there is evidence it may have also served as a fort. On June 7, 1663 the second of two wars started when the Esopus Indians set the village on fire. After a peace treaty was signed in 1664, the Esopus Indians gradually migrated from the area. From 1658 to 1677, the Stockade area was expanded three times to a perimeter of just under a mile. Now a National Historic District, it contains one of the largest clusters of 17th and 18th century Dutch style stone houses in the U.S.

(Kingston Marker)

House at 147 Green Street. The Dumond house, circa 1665, was likely given a Federal style makeover after the 1777 British torching. The architecture of the house is unique with so many split-levels that no two rooms are on the same level and the walls of the house are two feet thick.

Continue walking south to the intersection with John Street. In the southeast corner of the intersection is the Gerret Van Keuren House. The home was built around 1725 and was torched in 1777. Restored in the 1920's, its long, low structure is considered one of the best examples of Dutch style architecture in the stockade area.

Across the street from the Van Keuren House is the Colonel Abraham Hasbrouck House. Colonel Hasbrouck served with the

Northern Militia of Ulster County during the American Revolution and lived here from 1735 -1776.

Continue walking south on Green Street until you come to the intersection with Crown Street on the left. The home that is wedged between Crown and Green Streets is the Henry Sleight House and was built in the late 1600's. It is currently the headquarters of the

Judge Lucas Elmendorf Mansion

Built Circa 1790 by this regent, turnpike builder, associate of Thomas Jefferson. His election to congress 1797-1803 was celebrated by a grand illumination of this house 1798.

Friends of Historic
    Kingston 1967.

(Kingston Marker)

Wiltwyck Chapter of the Daughters of the American Revolution.

Just west of the Sleight House is the Judge Lucas Elmendorf III House. Judge Elmendorf was a three-term Congressman from 1797-1803 and a close associate of Thomas Jefferson. The home was built after the American Revolution around 1790.

Cornelius Tappen House

Was deputy county clerk in 1777 and saved many records when British burned Kingston. Reputedly the oldest house in Kingston and the first post office.

Friends of Historic
    Kingston 1976.

(Kingston Marker)

Just east of the Sleight House is the oldest surviving house in the stockade area, the Christopher Tappen House, was built around 1670. In 1777, Tappen was the Deputy County Clerk and is credited with saving the records of the county from the torch. The house later became the city's first post office.

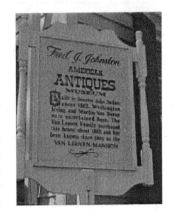

Continue walking south on Green Street to the intersection with Main Street. Walk east on Main Street until you reach the intersection with Wall Street. In the northeast corner of the intersection is the John Sudam House. The house built in the early 1800's includes Washington Irving and President Martin Van Buren as overnight guests. Today it is the Fred J. Johnston Museum and features 18th century furnishings and decorative arts. The museum is open from May to October.

The Old Dutch Church across the street from museum is the final stop on this walk around the stockade. Although the church was built in the 1850's, the congregation was organized in 1659. In 1777, the church was completely gutted by fire, but was repaired and used for another half century. The present church was constructed to house a growing congregation. Emphasizing the early struggles of the church, its motto is from Psalm 127:1 is: "Nis! Dominos Frustra" (Without the Lord all is in vain).

In the churchyard are gravestones dating from 1710. Stones bearing a St. Andrew's Cross identify some of the persons originally buried on the site of the present

The Reformed Protestant Dutch Church

This church organized in 1659 and chartered November 17, 1719 under His Majesty George King of Great Britain was served until December 1808 by pastors educated in the universities of Holland and Germany who preached in Dutch — the first sermon by the first pastor was delivered September 12, 1660 by whom the Lord's Supper was first administered. On the 26th of the following December, a minister's house was built in 1661 which subsequently was used both for religious duties and civil affaires. In 1679, a stone church was erected on the south-west corner of this lot which edifice was notably improved in 1721 and was rebuilt and dedicated November 26, 1752, N.S. The latter which is here represented was burned by the British, October 16, 1777 was renewed, extended in 1790 and was finally demolished in 1836. The next church was built of brick, dedicated August 20, 1833 and was located on the southeast corner of Wall and Main Streets. The last and present edifice (lecture-room on the north enlarged 1882) was dedicated September 28, 1852 during the pastorate of John Cantine Farrell Hoes, D.D., 1845-1867 to whose memory and that of his wife Lucy Maria Randall of Cortand New York, this tablet, as a record of the church and their association with it, is lovingly inscribed and presented by their daughter, Mary S. Hoes Burhans, Easter day 1900.

(Kingston Marker)

George Clinton

Born, July 26, 1739, Little Britain, N.Y. married February 7, 1770, Cornelia Tappen. Died April 20, 1812. Buried Washington, D. C. Ulster County Clerk, 1759-1812. Brigadier General, Revolutionary War. First Governor of New York State, 1777-1795, 1801-1804. Vice President of the United States under Jefferson and Madison, 1804-1812. Body and Monument brought to this site May 30, 1908.

To the memory of George Clinton. He was born in the state of New York on the 26th July 1739, and died at the city of Washington on the 20th April 1812, in the 73rd year of his age. He was a soldier and statesman of the Revolution, eminent in council, distinguished in war. He filled with unexampled usefulness, purity and ability, among many other high offices, those of Governor of his native state, and Vice President of the United States. While he lived, his virtue, wisdom, and valor were the pride, the ornament and security of his country, and when he died, he left an illustrious example of a well-spent life, worthy of all imitation. This m o n u m e n t   i s affectionately dedicated by his children.

(Kingston Marker)

church. Among the notable persons interred in the present churchyard is George Clinton, brigadier general in the Revolutionary War, first governor of New York State, and vice-president under Thomas Jefferson and James Madison. George Washington visited the church in 1782.

One other point of interest that you might also want to find is inside the stockade at the intersection of Crown and John Streets. This is the

1732 — 1932, In commemoration of the visit of

George Washington

To Kingston on the 16th of November 1782. His reception by the trustees of the free holders and commonality of the town and the consistory of this church, George J. L. Doll D.D., Dovinie. Levi Pawling, Abraham Klaarwater, Elders. Andries De Witt, Philip Hooghteyling, Deacons.

This tablet is erected by the people of Kingston on the 16th Day of November 1932. Franklin Delano Roosevelt, Governor of New York. Lucas Boeve, Dominie of the Church, Eugene Bernard Carey, Mayor of Kingston. Alphonso Trumpbour Clearwater, Chairman, W a s h i n g t o n B i c e n t e n n i a l Celebration Committee.

(Kingston Marker)

Van Deusen House

Built 1723, temporary capitol of state after burning of Kingston 1777.

NY State Historical Marker

(Hurley Marker)

only intersection in the United States where 18th century stone homes stand on all four corners.

Hurley — When the British terrorized Kingston, you might wonder where everyone fled to. The town of Hurley is about three miles from the Stockade. To reach the town, head west on Clinton Avenue which eventually turns onto the road to Hurley.

Hurley was settled in 1661. Like the Kingston Stockade, Hurley also has its share of eighteenth century stone houses. One house served as the senate building, thus

Old Guard House

Lieutenant David Taylor, British spy, was confined in this house and hanged on an apple tree, October 18, 1777.

State Education Department 1938

(Hurley Marker)

making Hurley also a former capital of New York State.

Overnight in Rhinebeck — A recommended spot for the evening is the Beekman Arms, which is across the Hudson River in Rhinebeck. Beekman Arms is the oldest, continually-operated inn in America and dates back to 1766. Although there is no record, George Washington purportedly reviewed the training of troops encamped in the area.

To get to the inn from the stockade, return back to the intersection with Pearl Street and turn left. Pearl Street will become Albany Street that will become Route 32. Stay on Route 32 until the intersection with NY 199

(about 12 miles from the Stockade). Follow 199 across George Clinton Kingston-Rhinecliff Bridge and turn right onto River Road (County Route 103) and follow it to its end at Rhinecliff Road (about 4 miles). Turn left onto Rhinecliff Road and follow it to the intersection with US Route 9 (about 1 mile). Beekman Arms is on the right. Reservations are recommended (914-876-7077).

BIBLIOGRAPHY

Bobrick, Benson, **Angel in the Whirlwind,** Penguin Books, New York, 1997.

Connolly, Courtney, Eileen Forrester and Jennifer Fragleasso, "Out & About," **Hudson Valley,** Volume XXIX, Number 1, Suburban Publishing, Poughkeepsie, NY 2000.

Fraunces Tavern Museum, "Fraunces Tavern Museum," New York, 2001.

Friends of Historic Kingston, "The Stockade Area of Kingston," Kingston, NY, 1997.

Gold, Nancy Dana, "Victory, by George," **Hudson Valley**, Volume XXVIII, No. 10, Suburban Publishing, Poughkeepsie, NY, 2000.

Keller, Allan, **Life Along the Hudson,** Lake Champlain Publishing Company, Burlington, VT, 1997.

Mid-Hudson Historic Consortium, "Historic Treasure of the Mid-Hudson Valley," Glenham, NY, 2001.

Office of Parks, Recreation and Historic Preservation, State of New York, "New Windsor Cantonment State Historic Site", 1995.

Office of Parks, Recreation and Historic Preservation, State of New York, "Senate House State Historic Site", 1999.

Office of Parks, Recreation and Historic Preservation, State of New York, "Washington's Headquarters State Historic Site", 1999.

Palisades Interstate Park Commission, "Fort Lee Historic Park,", Alpine, NJ, 2001.

Purcell, L. Edward and David F. Burg, Editors, **The World Almanac of the American Revolution**, Pharos

Books, New York, 1992.

Reformed Protestant Dutch Church, "Old Dutch Church," Kingston, NY, 2001.

Tappantown Historical Society, "Tappan, A Walk Through History," Tappan, NY, 2001.

Tappan Washington Memorial Corporation, Inc., "The George Washington Masonic Historic Site at Tappan, New York," Tappan, NY, 2001.

United States Military Academy, "West Point Museum," West Point, NY, 2001.

Raymond C. Houghton is a freelance historian and sole proprietor of Cyber Haus of Delmar, NY. He is a retired college professor, former government bureaucrat, Vietnam Veteran and one-time, General Electric employee. He has honors from the Department of Commerce, is listed in Who's Who in America and holds a doctorate from Duke University.